What others are saying about this book:

"Transforming analogies from a perfectly suited vessel for such timely insights! This is a demonstration of "Marketplace Grace" at its best. May we all be inspired to see parabolic insights about the Living God through our daily business as Wende has done.
A must read for all who thirst to know Christ more intimately!"

Pastor Terry Wayne Millender
Victorious Life Church, Alexandria, VA

"Serial entrepreneur and CEO Wende Jones has struck a rich vein of gold with this book, and has mined rich nuggets of wisdom, truth, revelation and practical application in the Spirit from her position as a technologist, software engineer/architect, and business executive.

This is a valuable resource for leaders everywhere. Wende is a world-class innovator and strategist, and now a world-class author. I recommend that you buy a copy for yourself and encourage others to do the same."

Dr. Bruce Cook
President, VentureAdvisers, Inc.

"In a dispensation when everything rises and falls on technology and there is a generation that communicates more in megabytes then sound bites *The God Port* could not be more relevant and appropriate.

Wende Jones is an example that all of us in the marketplace are called to be prophets and apostles within our various spheres of influence like Joseph, Nehemiah, Daniel and all those who came before us. Let he who has ears let him hear.

Patrice Tsague
Founder and Chief Servant Officer
Nehemiah Project International Ministries, Inc.

"Wende Jones has answered the age old question mankind has had for millennia...How do we communicate with God in a real, interactive way that allows us to not only express ourselves to Him but also to clearly hear Him?

Using computer technology as a contemporary illustration for effective communication with God, Wende points out the road blocks, hindrances, firewalls, etc we so often experience and shows how we can break through and have lively, interactive, life giving communication with God, 24 / 7."

"Wende uses her extensive knowledge of modern computer communication systems and in a very user friendly way that anyone can understand, draws easy to understand parallels of how to communicate with and hear from God as a lifestyle habit.

This is a must read for anyone wanting to deepen their walk with God through hearing His voice."

Michael Q. Pink
International speaker, business trainer, and best-selling author of Selling Among Wolves, *and* The Bible Incorporated.

The God Port

Accessing God in Real Time

Wende Jones

Elk Mountain Books, Wilsonville, Oregon

THE GOD PORT
Wende Jones

Published by:

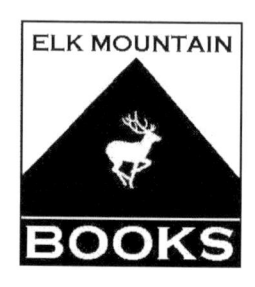

Elk Mountain Books
PO Box 21
Wilsonville, Oregon 97070
info@elkmountianbooks.com

All rights reserved. No part of this book may be reproduced or transmitted in any form or by any means, electronic or mechanical, including photocopying, recording or by any information storage and retrieval system without written permission from the author, except for the inclusion of brief quotations in a review.

Copyright © 2010 by Wende Jones

ISBN Print Edition: 1453706984
EAN-13: 9781453706985

Elk Mountain Books titles are available for special promotions and premiums. For details contact: sales@elkmountainbooks.com

Contents

Acknowledgements	7
Foreword	13
Preface	16
Overview	23
Introduction	27
1 Ports and Firewalls – *What is the God Port and how do our firewalls keep us from Him?*	29
2 Protocols and Bandwidth - *What protocol are you using and how much bandwidth do you have?*	41
3 Encryption and Decryption - *What is it and how does it work?*	55
4 Pings and Trace Routes – *Pursuing the God Port*	67
5 Uploads and Downloads – *How do we open the connection to the God Port?*	79
6 Search Engines and Keywords – *How do we learn about God and gain new insights?*	91
7 Dial up versus High-Speed - *How are we trying to connect?*	103
8 Page Cannot be Found? – *What are we missing?*	119
9 URL – *What's yours?*	127
10 Go back or continue - *What will you do next?*	135
11 SLA's and Uptime - *Is the return on investment worth it?*	143
12 Real-time Streaming – *What is God downloading?*	153
Afterword	163
About the Author	167
Scripture Listing	169

Acknowledgements

God brings many people into our lives, some for a lifetime some for a season and some for only a brief moment. However long I believe each encounter is no less important than the other if God is allowed to move through each one.

With that said there is no chance of me covering all the people by name I need to acknowledge that have brought me to this point in my life to write this book so for all of those who have crossed my path in a moment, for a season or for a lifetime, thank you for the enrichment you brought me and know that one way or another that encounter has contributed to this book.

My first thank you must go to God. The God Port book was given to me from God through The God Port! Praise God for His Holy Spirit, His son Jesus and His faithfulness. For His patience with me all these years and for His love that has sustained me in all things.

Next is my husband, Lance, who has stood beside me in all my adventures and allowed me to follow my passion for God, our children, my career and our businesses. He has never waivered in his support of me or belief in me. He is truly the wind behind my sails and the guard at my back! I could not have done all I have without his love, friendship, help and sacrifices.

He continues to teach me how to slow down, have fun, laugh more and enjoy all that is around me. I knew the moment I met him I would marry him someday and here we are! Thank you for all you do and always being there for me, I love you.

My children are each miracles from God and I cherish each one and they are absolutely delightful to be around and spend time with. They grew up too fast as all children do and I sacrificed too much time away from them and my husband in my career days but I get to spend the rest of my lifetime and eternity creating time with them.

Heather my youngest began this book adventure with me by transcribing my first notebook full of handwritten notes. Trust me that was no easy task considering my writing is worse than a doctor and even I can't read it half the time!

As we started I asked her to highlight the words she couldn't make out and just keep typing then we could go back over it and insert the words she missed. This didn't work for very long since there were more words highlighted on a page than not. We changed our approach and she kept transcribing and The God Port began to take shape.

The best part was the laughter we shared as we tried to make out my handwriting together pouring over the scribble that made up those first pages! Eventually through much encouragement from her I began typing my rough draft instead of handwriting which worked out best for all.

Thank you Heather, I love you!

Bre'anna, my first born, helped me wrap up the book by designing my book cover, she spent time pondering the design and considering the aspects of the book and how to portray those in the cover. She has always had a creative side and enjoyed some digital arts and communication classes in college this last year so we decided to put them to use.

It was great having her home for the summer and spending time with her. I enjoyed sharing the essence of the book with her and seeing her creativity and brilliance at work. We finally had something ready to show my editor and publisher and I was nervous he wouldn't like it. I was told the book cover is critical and needs to be done professionally but I just knew Bre'Anna was supposed to design it for me and could meet the challenge.

I thought it was fabulous and so did my publisher! With a few more edits and suggested changes we were off and running.

Thank you Bre'Anna, I love you!

So my last born helped me start and my first born helped finish which brings a smile to a mother's face and tears to her eyes. My husband kept things going in the middle encouraging me, carving out quiet time for me when I needed to write and pulling me away from my laptop when I needed a break.

It was definitely a family affair in so many ways! Our other daughter, Stephanie, busied herself raising our grandchildren who bring a joy all of their own.

My mom has truly been my lifelong fan and cheering section. She always told me I could do anything I put my mind to and even when I had given up on myself she did not! If I could have one wish for the world it would be that all children could have a mom like mine. Frankly, she was mom to many as my sisters and I grew up.

Our friends always came to our house and mom welcomed each one and she was mom to many over the years. My daughters' friends call me Mama Jones which makes me hopeful that I have somehow carried on what my mom started. When she remarried I didn't gain a "step-father" I gained a second dad, Louie or Ole LP I call him for short (another story). He had no idea what he was getting into with our family but he has rolled with the punches every step of the way and our lives have been all the more enriched.

Thank you both, I owe you more than time or money could ever repay!

My sisters Robyn and Cindy have stood by me no matter what, through thick and thin they were there to love me, pray for me and lift me before the Lord when I couldn't do it myself and I pray I have been there for them since then.

Again, a whole book here so let me just say thank you to you both and your husbands and my nieces (yes lots of girls in the family) and nephew-in-law for your unfailing love and support and nights around the family game table together! I love you all.

Not last or least is my Nana who is a wealth of wisdom, experience and a barrel of laughs. I love to hear the stories of old as she tells them and shares our family history with us as well as the funny thing that happened this morning! Sometimes with a smile and sometimes with a tear but always with a strength and steadfastness that comes from living a long life and persevering through what ever comes your way.

I love you Nana, I forgive you for the unwanted haircut when I was five!

This book is also in fond memory of my dad, my Aunty Nor, my brother Johnny and my second mom, Wanda (fondly known as Grandma Wanda to my children) who have left marks on my life that I will carry and cherish always. Michelle, thank you for sharing your mom unselfishly with us all and you're sisterly advice over the years.

Sisters are more than blood and you have always been there for us all just as your mom was!

My dad is in heaven already singing and dancing with the angels and raising a bit of a ruckus I would suspect. Shortly after he passed away God gave me a vision of daddy up in heaven dancing with the angels and smiling like I had never seen him smile when he was here on earth and it still gives me great joy today.

He was always my supporter and whether near or far away I always knew he loved me and was thinking about me. He was actually the writer in the family and I thank him for whatever small talent I may have because of his joy he found in it. He wrote each of my sisters and I a song when we were born and sang it to us when we were little, when we traveled we always sang fun little songs and he made up great big stories (pink elephants and purple giraffes were common characters) to entertain us!

Special thanks to Tammy Cinnera, John Kelly, Patrice Tsague and Perry Perkins. Tammy my office manager for encouraging me every step of the way and helping with the final edits and reviews.

John for sharing his years of wisdom and experience in the writing world with me and helping me prepare the book proposal and chapter titles and overview. His direction kept me moving and improving the book as I fine tuned my message and my delivery of that message. His initial encouragement as I shared the book was confirmation that the topic was timely and fresh which inspired me to keep going.

Patrice for sharing his wisdom and experience with self-publishing and directing my final steps to get this book to print. His encouragement and support as my business coach and my friend have been invaluable over these past few years.

Perry you have been a true answer to prayer for moving me through the self-publishing process as you took on the role of editor and publisher for me. Your advice, wisdom and guidance have made the process fun and exciting. God willing I look forward to more adventures together with future books!

Finally to my staff, friends, clients, colleagues, coaches and prayer partners, thank you all!

Foreword

During my life, I have learned that there are many voices competing in my own heart and mind.

I am referring to the influences of parents, family, friends, the media, my own voice, and numerous others. Most of the time I can sort them out, but sometimes it is hard for me to discern where I learned something to be from my own or the impression another person has made upon my soul.

After ten years in full time ministry I found myself in a season of division and difficulty. The confusion was so overwhelming, and I desperately needed direction.

It was throughout that period I began to learn that there is to be *One* voice above all the others, and I am not talking about my own. In fact, as I learned to hear the loving and healing voice of my Lord, I wondered out loud why the church had been so negligent in teaching me how to be confident in hearing His voice.

The Scriptures are full of promises and stories of people who heard the voice of the Lord specifically and clearly. Jesus told us in John 10:3-4, *"The watchman opens the gate for him, and the sheep listen to his voice. He calls his own sheep by name and leads them out. When he has brought out all his own, he goes on ahead of them, and his sheep follow him because they know his voice."* (NIV)

These verses are explicitly about an intimate relationship of hearing clearly the voice of the Shepherd. How did we lose the expectation to hear God with total confidence?

When I met Wende Jones, I sensed something very different about her.

She was involved in a church, but that wasn't her main identity as a believer. She spoke specifically of how God revealed Himself to her in a personal and powerful way.

Even though she was formerly in a traditional church setting, she was living out the reality of how to know God in a deep and profound fashion. It was not about religion or performance for her, but how to touch, and be touched, by the One who calls us by name.

In the late 1990's Wende began to attend the church where I was the Senior Pastor. She had such a sincerity and eagerness about her. In essence, she was hungering after the presence of God. Nothing was more important to Wende than sitting at Jesus feet and discovering His vision and purpose for her life.

The Spirit put it on my heart to conduct a series of classes at the church to help people discover their destiny. The Lord also led me to invite Wende to be a part of one of six week sessions.

During that season she shared with us that the Lord would release her into public ministry and speaking.

What would be her message?

For her, it was about how to love God with all of your heart, mind, soul, and strength. Therefore, it comes as no surprise to me that Wende has now entered into that ministry!

The God Port is creatively written in the vernacular of the day, which is the language of ports, websites, and social networking.

In these pages Wende draws insightful analogies and parallels from the World Wide Web. However, the life in the pages is the means to draw you into the heart of God and how to hear His voice clearly. For Wende, the goal is not just to hear God, but to experience the radical and passionate love that He has for each one of us.

So, if you long to know Him, far beyond what you know and the voices all around you, prepare yourself to enter into a relationship that will heal and transform you in the deepest places of your inner man.

Don't hold back…enter into the God port and discover the place where you know His voice and experience all He has for you!

Dr. Mark Tubbs

Executive Director of Harvest International Ministries, Int'l Vice-Chancellor of the Wagner Leadership Institute.

Preface

I always knew and accepted there was a God and thinking about Him came naturally to me.

I remember as early as five years old playing outside and talking with God as if He was right there and my best friend and telling Him I would be the first woman president!

In Junior High I sought out more about what this meant and who He really was. I gave my life to the Lord in high school but struggled with my walk because I didn't know how to personalize it.

I was going through the motions but there didn't seem to be any real life in it for me.

Looking back I realize the focus was on salvation as the end which was not satisfying or meaningful and the worldly view and pressures eventually won out.

I graduated from the University of Oregon in 1983 with a double major in management and finance and began exploring the different business segments and markets to find what I enjoyed doing. But my life took a turn for the worse, my dreams of a career and success faded as I tumbled into darkness from drugs, alcohol and an abusive co-dependent relationship.

By late 1989 my life circumstances were tragic and painful, the threat of death had passed by me several times and I had a decision to make, give my life back to God or lose my life. I had a brand new baby that was counting on me and I had to make a life for her, if not for me.

In the late hours of one night, in a desolate and frightening environment I called out to God in a way I had never done or known before and He answered me. His light filled my surroundings, his peace came at a time when one would least expect it and my commitment grew strong.

No matter what I would never give Him up again!

The road back was long and hard, there were many life changing obstacles that stood before me and broken relationships needed to be healed along with many years of deep wounding. I had consequences I had to face for my poor decisions and getting mixed up with the wrong crowd.

I was a single mom, with a brand new baby, facing a trail of destruction (another story for another book another time!)

Yet, God was and is faithful and He performed miracle after miracle in my life and I didn't miss one birthday of my daughter's life and celebrated the birth of my second daughter a few short years later. My strength came from God's promise in Philippians 4:13 and has been the sustaining verse for my life every since.

> *"I can do all things through Christ which strengtheneth me."*

Today I have a wonderful husband, three fabulous children and four grandchildren and a fifth one on the way, each and everyone a miracle from God.

My greatest joy has always been and will remain my relationship with God and my family.

I worked a lot of hours to climb the corporate ladder but committed every other moment to my family, not wanting to miss anymore than I had to. My girls would come to the office with me on Saturdays and we had some great times. They would setup their office in the large, fancy boardroom while I completed my work. They built forts under the conference table and wrote out their very large tax bills on the white board.

I loved having them with me and learned the best I could to balance my corporate career with my family life. As my children grew older I began to wonder what my purpose was outside of raising a family and working a lot!

I had always been a hard worker and strived for excellence in all things. The redemptive quality of work has been a significant factor in my life and long before I realized that was God's intention.

As my walk with God deepened I began wondering about what God had for me, what was His purpose for my life, what was my ministry to the world?

The idea of going "into the ministry full-time" and leaving the marketplace never resonated with my spirit yet that's what people were supposed to do! How could I do God's work and stay in the work place? I started bible studies at my work, shared God with co-workers and prayed with people whenever the opportunity arose but continued to wonder about "full-time ministry."

God began to show me the importance of my work in the marketplace and that was indeed my full-time ministry.

I had worked in healthcare for several years when an opportunity to explore technology arose to solve some immediate business problems.

I was hooked!

The technology came alive and I immediately realized the power of computers, databases and business applications for improving business processes and productivity. I eventually sought out a career in technology and landed at a small software development company that was just in the stage of moving into the web technology and writing software for the internet.

In a few short years I was running the business and managing all aspects of the operations as well as consulting directly with clients for their technology needs. It was time to take my years of business management and technology experience and start my own business where I would be free to build the business according to my morals and principles, unconstrained by a "boss" and their worldview.

After working for others for many years it was time for me to build a business with Christ, His way.

I loved technology and learning about new businesses and helping businesses adapt technology to meet their needs, and I've always loved a good challenge and so I launched my own business, God's business in 2004 with my loving family supporting and encouraging me the whole way.

It was exciting and frightening all at the same time, but God as always was faithful and guided me through each turn, each decision, each crisis and each victory!

But still, there was something missing, the greater purpose for my existence!

I began to have more questions than answers and desperately wanted to do what He had called me to, but what exactly was that?

I wanted to be obedient in all things, but which voice in my head was His?

How could I be obedient if I couldn't distinguish His voice from my own, the world and the influences around me?

I sought out other marketplace leaders at conferences and through devotionals and books. I needed to know what God's vision was for my life. I had seen glimpses of much but had not progressed on any one thing.

At a conference in 2008 I was talking with one of the young women speakers and I told her I wanted to do so much for

God but didn't know where to start. She said bluntly, "spend more time with God, He will show you."

How dare she think I don't spend enough time with God, I thought, but you know what? I didn't.

I went to church, I went to conferences, I read my bible occasionally, and I tithed. I was doing all the Christian *things* I was supposed to but was I really spending quality, quiet time with God? I had to answer no to that question and I knew I was at a cross roads.

So, I could continue on the merry-go-round of life I felt I was on, or I could do something about it. I decided right then that I would spend more time with God and press in to who He was.

I remember praying and telling God I didn't know how and He said, I will teach you. This is where my God Port journey began and it is still a journey that I pursue and cherish.

Am I perfect, no, am I persistent yes!

As I began to really, truly spend time with God and press in to Him, He poured into me His purposes, provided mentors and access to leaders already ministering in the marketplace and my vision began to grow and take shape. As a Christian business owner I needed to set the standards, build my business according to God's principles and truly stand apart.

This would give me opportunities to share with others why my business was different, why I could succeed where others failed and how by the grace of God I had arrived at this place.

God was preparing me for the economic fall, the uncertain times and grounding me in His word and path so that I might "press on toward the goal for which I had been called."

God was preparing me to write this book, His book to lift up and encourage others to truly "seek Him with their whole heart". I am still learning what this means and God is faithful in teaching us as we press into Him.

I hope you enjoy The God Port and you begin your own journey with God, seeking all He has for you.

Overview

Do God's people hear His voice? Are they directly connected? How often are they plugged in?

The God Port is my journey in learning how to hear God's voice and my desire to help others do the same. People now more than ever need to be seeking God's direction and revelation for their lives. God is shaking the foundations of the earth to gain His children's attention and focus. As the economic climate continues to shift causing fear and discomfort in the lives of the believer and the non-believer many will seek God for answers.

Will you be the Salt and Light you are called to be, step into your calling and election and bring Honor and Glory to God?

I believe you want to or you wouldn't be reading this book. But if you cannot hear the voice of God, you cannot follow His commands and be sure of your calling and election. You cannot act in faith and obedience if you are second guessing His voice and direction in your life. The Port 3303 analogy comes from *Jeremiah 33:03, "Call to me and I will answer you and tell you great and unsearchable things you do not know."* My pastor always referred to this as God's phone number so as I began my journey to hear God's voice, I started here. Calling God and listening for answers as His word promises.

The God Port uncovers my journey to hear God's voice, to dwell in His word, to "press" in to who He is and who I am in Him so I can step into my calling and election I am predestined for. More importantly I hope by sharing this journey, the trials and errors and pitfalls I went through that you will be encouraged and directed to do the same and hopefully avoid a few of the obstacles I encountered.

For you that have not yet decided to pursue God, I pray you will make that decision and begin to understand the love the Father has for you.

What is the God Port, how does it work and how can it help us draw nearer to God and hear His voice more readily and with confidence?

The use of the word "port" is an analogy to the internet and the flow of information. A port can provide one way or two-way communication; it can be slightly open and allow just a small amount of information in or wide open allowing a constant flow of information back and forth. If a port is slightly open information can get lost because there is not enough "bandwidth" or "throughput" to allow the information to flow seamlessly.

Have you ever accessed a website and gotten an error message like "page cannot be displayed", "page cannot be found" or "page has been moved"?

This is how I felt when trying to hear God's voice and receive critical information regarding important decisions in my life. I wanted to be obedient to what He was asking me to do but wasn't sure if it in deed was His voice!

Information was spotty at best, slow to download or lost altogether and I was frustrated. It was time to pull out all the stops and get my God Port opened wide for consistent, two-way information!

But, the question was how.

I began with pursuing God and seeking Him with all my heart. I began "pressing" in to who He was and who I was in Him which led me directly in to the God Port and learning to hear His voice.

The pursuit of hearing God's voice started with really spending time with God and reading His word. If you want to get to know an author you read their books, you begin to understand how they think and what they do or what their characters do.

So, if you want to get to know God you need to read His word and get to know Him better and understand what His characters do (Adam, Noah, Abraham, Moses, David, Esther, Jesus, etc..).

To begin to understand Him and understand how He thinks and what He might do in certain situations and to learn from the characters in His book. As you do this you begin to really believe what His word says is true which for me has opened up a world of possibilities I didn't think existed. One of which is writing this book.

I invite you to join me in my journey so you may launch your own journey and find out what possibilities await you as you pursue God with all your heart and learn to open…

The God Port.

Introduction

The God Port is a book after God's own heart.

I have spent the last few years pursuing God in a way I have never done before. God pressed upon my heart the need to spend more time with Him and learn to hear His voice (without doubt) and understand His heart in a deeper way than ever before.

He called me to "prepare myself" for "a time such as this."

I didn't know what was coming only that I wanted to be in-tune and in-step with what God was doing.

So, my journey began.

As I began on this pursuit, I realized I had a lot to learn about spending time with God, hearing His voice and staying plugged in throughout the day to hear His wisdom and revelation as I needed it, in the exact moment I needed it.

My goal became not only to hear His voice but to know His voice and stay plugged in, connected and receiving revelation 24/7, ever increasing the bandwidth between God and I, making sure not to "drop" any packets or worse using only one-way communication again!

Jesus always taught in parables to help "enlighten the eyes of our understanding." I hope you will find the same to be true in this book as I share my journey with some fun technology analogies God brought to light along the way.

Not many of us are farmers and fishermen anymore but most of us have computers and use the internet in our day-to-day lives so technology examples seemed applicable for today's readers.

Now, for you technology guru's - remember we are keeping it simple and building some general analogies...so don't hang me out to dry on the lack of technical details or proficiency!

At the end of each chapter I have added a "walking it out" section to help conceptualize what I just covered by giving examples of my journey in this area. This book comes directly from The God Port and is proof that God keeps His promises and blesses us with His wisdom and divine visitation as we press in and open our God Port.

The things written here are the experiences of what God has taught me which means they work and will work for you too!

So settle in, enjoy reading the God Port and begin your journey.

I can't wait to hear about it!

Chapter One

Ports and Firewalls - What is the God Port and how do our firewalls keep us from Him?

"**Call to me** *and I will answer you and tell you great and unsearchable things you do not know.*" - Jeremiah 33:03

While growing up my pastor always referred to this scripture as God's phone number. When we would ask questions of him he would refer us to this scripture and tell us to get God on the phone and ask Him.

We were teenagers so the idea of this was exciting – chatting on the phone with God (today teens would probably "Skype" God).

When asked by our friends the next day what we did last night we could casually say, "Oh we just chatted on the phone with God!" However the actual mechanics of how it could really work escaped me and the "belief" that God wanted to chat with me at all was not active in my walk at that time.

As God began to call me into a deeper place with Him in recent years and I began to ask Him how, this scripture came flooding back and I knew it was time to dig in and understand what this meant and how to do it.

I asked God with an expectation of Him answering me and He began to unravel His mysteries to me in a way I could relate to, technology!

In technology terms a port is an open line of communication where information can pass through once permission is given and the firewall rules are set.

A firewall can be thought of as a brick wall and to pass information through you have to "punch through" the firewall by removing a brick to provide an opening to that port. In other words you need a rule in the firewall to get through a specific port number.

You have to know the port number to setup the rule in the firewall and setup the permissions to remove the brick.

There are many well-known or standard port numbers used in internet communications so that the communication can be established and the firewall rules can be set.

For instance the common port to allow traffic from the internet to a particular server is port 80. Everyone that hosts websites has a rule in their firewall that allows internet traffic to come through on port 80. The common port for allowing files to be transferred to a server is the FTP (file transfer protocol) port known as port 20 or 21. The port that handles all the DNS (Domain Name System) traffic is port 53, so if you are using a server to host and look up domain names you have to allow traffic to come through port 53. In each of these cases the port number has to be first identified, and then entered into the firewall with a set of permissions to allow access.

The above verse in Jeremiah is referring to the port that needs opened between us and God.

What does it take to open this port? A simple phone call!

"Call to me," the verse says and "I will answer you."

Port 3303 refers to calling God on His phone number, His direct line ... The God Port!

The first step to opening a port and entering permissions to access it in the firewall is to know the right port number.

Now we know God's port number 3303 and guess what, there is currently no "well-known" function already assigned to this port number in the standard lists of ports. Is that significant? Maybe not, but God's hand is in everything and He is a God of details so I don't take this as a coincidence but confirmation that we are on the right port.

So while this port number is not amongst the well-known standards in the computing world, I believe it is well known in the heavenly realms and for those of us that read God's word and understand it this verse clearly identifies God's phone number, port 3303, The God Port.

> *"Look at the birds of the air; they do not sow or reap or store away in barns, and yet your heavenly Father feeds them. Are you not much more valuable than they?"* Matthew 6:26

You are worth much more than that, God said in Luke.

To open the God Port we must begin to believe scripture and what God says about who we are in Him. We need to set aside the lies that have been rolling around in our head all these years and begin believing the truths of God. As we quiet those voices of inadequacy, guilt, shame and worthlessness we can begin to hear what God is saying to us and about us.

This is the beginning of opening the God Port, believing we are who God says we are. We will talk about this in more detail later in the book because it is critical to our success but for now let's finish laying the foundations for the God Port.

Now that we have the right port number, Port 3303, call to me, what's next?

We have to address the firewalls that block our flow of communication in the God port. What is our firewall that needs opened to allow the communication between us and God? What is God's firewall that allows communication from Him to us?

Remember there are firewalls on both ends of the communication, and we need to address them both.

Our firewall could be considered our heart and mind and what we believe. Our firewall is where the "rules" of communication live, our rules based on what we know and what we believe to be true.

What bricks do you have in place keeping you from accessing all God has for you?

God gave me a vision of my firewall, literally a brick wall standing between Him and me. On these bricks were written all the things I believed about myself over the years, all the messages that had come to me from the world instead of from Him. He began to show me how to remove these bricks by speaking His truths (His living word) to them and to myself. This was not a speedy process by any means; this is the pressing in and persevering part of the journey.

We have to allow God time to work with us and remove the bricks, one by one.

What are your bricks that are keeping you from opening the God Port and receiving what God has for you?

Bricks of inadequacy, bricks of guilt and shame, bricks of pride, bricks of doubt, bricks of past sins, bricks of current sins or maybe bricks of mistrust and unbelief. What ever they are they can be removed as you experience the true love of the Father.

> *"How great is the love the Father has lavished on us, that we should be called children of God! And that is what we are! The reason the world does not know us is that it did not know him.* I John 3:1

So, if our heart and mind are our firewall what is God's firewall?

Jesus says this, *"I am the way and the truth and the life. No one comes to the Father except through me. If you really knew me, you would know my Father as well. From now on, you do know him and have seen him." (John 14:6-7)*

God's word says that no one comes to the Father except through His Son. Jesus goes on to say that if we know him we will know the Father.

This makes Jesus the firewall to God.

> *"I tell you the truth, the Son can do nothing by himself; he can do only what he sees his Father doing, because whatever the Father does the Son also does." John 5:19*

Jesus is always in direct communication with the Father, so the ports are wide open between God and Jesus and between Jesus and the Holy Spirit.

So, really our concern is two fold:

First, having a right relationship with Jesus (which we will discuss in more depth later) since He is the only way to the Father.

Second, opening the port between us and the Holy Spirit within us so we can hear God's voice.

> *"If anyone is thirsty, let him come to me and drink. Whoever believes in me, as the Scripture has said, streams of living water will flow from within him." John 7:37-38*

This is the Holy Spirit communicating with us and flowing from within us. This verse goes on to read, ""*By this he meant the Spirit, whom those who believed in him were later to receive. Up to that time the Spirit had not been given, since Jesus had not yet been glorified.*"

This was written before the day of Pentecost, before Jesus had been glorified and seated at the right hand of God. Now, however, we live in the days *after* Pentecost, after the Holy Spirit had been sent by God, so we can walk and flow in the Holy Spirit all of our days. Let's make sure you got that, where are the living waters flowing from?

Where is the Holy Spirit residing? From within us!

The wisdom and revelation that is coming from God through Jesus to the Holy Spirit and into our hearts is the open port, the direct connection, The God Port! We just need to learn how to open the flow of communication and remove the "bricks" that are blocking the flow.

Are we opening this port to God?

If not, why not?

What is stopping us from truly hearing, seeing and walking in what God is calling us to by opening this port? Is it fear, doubt and disbelief?

My guess is that it is all of these things but it is also because we haven't learned how to dial up Gods phone number, open our port 3303 and begin removing the bricks in our firewall?

Maybe you don't believe there is a God Port? Let's make sure we address that right now.

After the fall of man in the garden, God removed himself from the earth and from man's access. Only a certain few heard God's voice and were found "righteous" before him to do so. The God port was closed except to just a select few.

After Jesus came to earth to die for our sins and forgive us our sins Jesus promised us God would not leave us again.

Jesus said, *"I tell you the truth, anyone who has faith in me will do what I have been doing. He will do even greater things than these, because I am going to the Father."* John 14:12

Jesus says again in John 16:7, *"But I tell you the truth: It is for your good that I am going away. Unless I go away, the Counselor will not come to you; but if I go, I will send him to you.*

"But the Counselor, the Holy Spirit, whom the Father will send in my name, will teach you all things and will remind you of everything I have said to you. John 14:26

The "Counselor" is the Holy Spirit.

Jesus died and went to be with the Father and He said we would do greater things than He, because we were being filled with the Holy Spirit and He would teach us and remind us of everything Jesus said. We were redeemed back to God and given His Holy Spirit so that we would always be in touch and in communion with God the Father and the Son through the Holy Spirit.

The God Port was opened up again and the direct communication from God in Heaven to His children here on Earth was restored.

How are you hearing God?

What is He saying to you?

Are you listening?

God is always speaking, always sharing His heart and always communing with us through His Holy Spirit that He left here on earth for us, in us.

We just need to learn how to open our God Port and get connected and plugged in!

Walking it Out

Hearing God's voice is not a new concept, nor is having the Holy Spirit within us.

I have been a believer for most of my life and have been actively walking out my faith since I recommitted my life to the Lord over 20 years ago.

However, in all those years I never really mastered hearing God's voice consistently and without doubt. Sure there were times I knew I was hearing Him and He was giving me direction and guidance but there were more times that I was not hearing Him.

He performed miracle after miracle in my life (which is for another book) yet I struggled to hear Him clearly and to be able to stand in His presence.

Throughout most of those years I can honestly say that I was lacking in the very areas we are going to cover in this book which is why my God Port was not opened until these past few years.

I spent years feeling bad in church on Sunday because I had not done all I knew I should for the Lord during the week.

I spent more time beating myself up about what I wasn't doing than just getting started doing something. I was on Satan's play ground!

The teeter totter ... up and down and up and down thinking being on top was the answer but as soon as Satan put his foot down you were left hanging high and dry and unable to move.

The merry-go-round...working all week to make ends meet, going to church on Sunday to get refreshed only to end up back on the merry-go-round Monday morning right back in the same spot you left on Friday!

The slide...climbing the ladder of success to reach the top, but finding out it was a quick, slick, slide down the other side.

The swing...getting a running start to jump in and start pumping your legs for all you are worth to get really high in the sky then as soon as you quit moving you came to a halt and had to start over.

If you have ever been on this playground or find your self here now then keep reading!

The principles you will learn in this book on how to open the God port are the principles I used to get off the merry-go-round and stay off, bale out of the swing and keep flying, slide down the slide and find a ladder on the other end and pin Satan to the ground...and hold him there!

Action Items

Reflect: What came to mind regarding bricks in your firewall while you were reading this chapter? Did something specific come to mind? What are you going to do to remove it so you can open The God Port? Is God speaking to you right now?

_____
_____
_____
_____
_____
_____
_____
_____
_____

Pray: *Lord thank you for this reader and their heart to get to know you better. God you know what they are thinking about right now and you want to meet them right here where they are. Lord while we see the inadequacies of our lives and our shortcomings and faults and let them hold us back, You do not.*

Lord you only ever see us perfected in You and You are standing at the ready to pour out Your love upon this reader. Let Your Holy Spirit move upon them and refresh them and free them from their bricks so they might see You more clearly and know You love them.

Do: Write one of your bricks you identified and just released to God in the space below, now visualize ripping it up and throwing it over your shoulder!

It is gone, it is behind you, and it is finished. The only one that has permission to bring it back to the front is you, so refuse to give it space or time in your life.

If you feel it creeping to the front just visualize yourself throwing it over your shoulder and send it packing!

Firewall Brick:

_____

Write: Write out your thoughts below. What was God showing you and speaking to you? Just start writing and allow the Holy Spirit to flow through you. One word, one sentence, one paragraph whatever comes to mind.

_____
_____
_____
_____
_____
_____
_____
_____

Chapter Two

Protocols and Bandwidth: What protocol are you using and how much bandwidth do you have?

In the first chapter, we talked about ports and firewalls and how those related to the God Port. The other piece of our God Port is to know what type of port to dial into in order to establish the right type of communication with God and to allow an adequate opening to receive all God has for us.

Many of us have a one-way communication going with God.

God I need, God I want, God please help, God fix this, God do that...sound familiar? I have spent years saying prayers like this but they are one-way and short-sighted. What God is promising us in Jeremiah 33:03 is two-way communication, ***"Call to me*** (that's our part) *and* ***I will answer you*** *and tell you great and unsearchable things you do not know"* (this is God's part).

We are missing out on the best part when we only open one-way communication; we are missing all the best stuff from God, His answers, His direction, His revelation and His heart for us and what He has called us to!

What type of port protocol are you opening with God, is it one-way or two-way communication?

Here are the two basic protocols that I think address our communication with God.

Can you recognize which one you use most often?

TCP	UDP
Transmission Control Protocol (TCP) is a connection-oriented protocol, which means that it **requires handshaking** to set up end-to-end communications. Once a connection is set up user data may be sent **bi-directionally** over the connection.	User Datagram Protocol (UDP) is a simpler **message-based connectionless protocol**. Connectionless protocols do not set up a dedicated end-to-end connection. Communication is achieved by **transmitting information in one direction from source to destination** without verifying the readiness or state of the receiver.
Reliable	Unreliable
Ordered	Not Ordered
Heavyweight	Lightweight
Streaming	Datagrams / Packets

Do you see that?

The UDP is called a connectionless, simple message-based protocol.

If we are opening our God Port we are saying we want to connect with God but how can we do this if we are using a connectionless protocol.

I have been using the wrong method for years! Yet, God is faithful even in this and managed to break through the barriers and drive me to a protocol that offered an end-to-end connection. Praise God!

TCP ports (Transmission Control Protocol) enable two hosts to establish a connection and exchange streams of data once the firewall is open. TCP guarantees delivery of data and that those packets will be delivered in the same order in which they were sent.

If we are opening a port to God don't we want a guarantee of delivery and two way communication and getting it sent in the right order would be helpful!

I have spent the last several years seeking this open communication, hungering for this direct connection and wondering why God wasn't speaking to me! Of course, He was speaking and is always speaking I just didn't hear Him because I was using the wrong port protocol, the wrong communication method.

I was using the simple messaging protocol port (UDP) which is considered one-way, unreliable communication instead of using the TCP communication which enables two-way, end-to-end communication.

The simple messaging protocol did not allow for God to communicate back to me through His Holy Spirit because I was too busy sending out massive one way messages! Sound familiar?

The eyes of my heart have truly been enlightened. This is so simple but so revelatory, we have to get on the right protocol.

I think that, as believers, our first mistake is thinking when we don't hear God it's because He is not speaking. I think it's much more likely that we are not listening to the Holy Spirit within us (God's messenger.)

Why?

Because we are using the wrong communication protocol for opening our port. His messages cannot get through because we have tied up all the bandwidth with our own words!

We have tied up what, our *bandwidth*…what is this?

Bandwidth refers to how much information can be passed back and forth based on the width or size of the opening.

So, if we think about opening our God port we are talking about the line of communication being open both ways (TCP) and widening the tunnel (bandwidth) in which the communication can pass.

If the port is only open one direction you only get one way communication, you're speaking to God but He is not speaking back. So once we get the port open for two way communication then we want to increase the width of the opening, the pipe, the tunnel so more information can pass through.

The wider tunnel also allows for faster throughput therefore more information in less time and no slowdowns due to lack of capacity!

Bandwidth is defined as a measure of available or consumed data communication resources and **throughput** is the average rate of successful message delivery over a communication channel.

The idea of bandwidth implies both availability of space to pass data as well as the capacity to consume the data.

How much room there is in the tunnel to send information back and forth and how much capacity is available to consume the information sent. What this means is that we can have enough bandwidth to receive the data sent but we might not have enough capacity to consume it.

Consuming means to absorb or to eat or drink up.

Here is the clincher; God will not send us more data than we have the capacity to consume!

So for years I was praying for more from God but He knew I didn't have the capacity to consume it yet, to absorb it, to drink it up.

For instance if we think about a website, some websites get a lot of "traffic" and some get only a little "traffic."

If we define traffic as the number of visitors coming to "consume" the information on the website then in this case the website with more visitors is consuming more information and both take more bandwidth.

Both websites might have the same amount of bandwidth available to send and receive data but only one of the websites is "consuming" up to their capacity. So, how are we doing with our information from God?

Are we sending and receiving all we can?

Are we consuming all He is offering us, or is our capacity under utilized?

God will not expand our bandwidth until we begin to consume all He is already sending us!

> *"How precious to me are your thoughts, O God! How vast is the sum of them! Were I to count them, they would outnumber the grains of sand. When I awake, I am still with you."* - Psalm 139:17-18

If we are using up all our bandwidth to send our prayers and requests to God, what is left for Him to return His thoughts to us that outnumber the grains of sand?

God is always speaking but our bandwidth is sometimes maxed out with our own thoughts and we have no more capacity to consume what He is trying to relay to us.

We are not always tuned in because we are too busy listening to ourselves! We also get distracted with the noise of the world and if we don't press into God we can't hear the sweet, subtle voice of our Father.

Remember, He gives us a choice and if we choose the noise of the world or ourselves He will allow us not to hear Him but He is still speaking, whispering, and wooing us as a voice from afar; calling us to Him.

Now hang in there with me on this; I want to take it one step further...

Bandwidth can be utilized in "fixed" increments or "bursts."

For those websites that have received a lot of traffic over time but some days experience "lulls" in the action they will utilize "burstable" bandwidth. This automatically increases the size of the tunnel to allow for the increased traffic as it happens real-time and avoids the "slowdowns" that could be experienced if their bandwidth was "fixed" and their capacity was overloaded thus being unable to consume any further requests.

What kind of bandwidth do you have with God?

Is it fixed, so you only consume so much or is it burstable allowing for real-time increases in capacity as God chooses to download more to you to consume?

If we let our history of low capacity and one way communication dictate our fixed bandwidth we will miss the "bursts" God sends us.

We must increase our capacity to consume, so God will send more.

I have spent years allowing God to operate within my limited size, fixed bandwidth settings I have put on Him all the while asking Him for more but not expanding my capacity to receive it. I have remained in that fixed bandwidth tunnel size that gives me just enough information that I can comfortably understand and consume.

Never believing or having faith for more from God and never stretching myself to something more.

If we ask God for more, we must increase our bandwidth for consumption, we must be open to all God has for us that will come when we are dialed in to our God Port so as our capacity to consume increases then our bandwidth can "burst open" to allow for the increase!

That increase will come from the Holy Spirit imparting the things of God to us as we stand at the ready. It's an exciting adventure and requires us to remove the limitations we have put on ourselves and on God.

Let's dig in deeper on this idea of burstable bandwidth, it's an exciting revelation and deserves a closer look.

God is a God of amazement and wonder, the sooner we receive that and believe that the sooner we will be ready to increase our bandwidth and open the port and begin bursting with the things of God.

What does burst actually mean and how does that apply to our communication with God?

Well let's go to dictionary.com and check it out (when was the last time anyone used the 10 pound printed Webster dictionary to look up a word?)

Burst means ...

- ... to break, break open, or fly apart with sudden violence: *If we define violence as "swift and intense force" we can see how this applies to our opening of our God Port. We are breaking old thoughts, old patterns and letting them fly apart with swift and intense force to allow the things of God to "burst" forth.*

- ... to issue forth suddenly and forcibly, as from confinement or through an obstacle: *What are the obstacles we have held up to block God in our life? What are the bricks in the firewall we have put in place to keep Him out and us comfortable? Remove them and experience God bursting through! Through your thoughts, through your dreams, through your daily priorities. He is waiting, patiently and lovingly to burst upon the scene.*

... to give sudden expression to or as if to emotion: *to burst into applause; to burst into tears. Trust me there will be plenty of applause and tears in this process of opening your God port and letting God truly order your life. But the emotion of not doing it is worse, frustration, loneliness, lack of hope, joy, righteousness and peace in your life. These are the things God promises us, open your God Port, increase your bandwidth and let the things of God burst out of you instead of your temper and frustration.*

... to be extremely full, as if ready to break open: *God is bursting with joy and excitement as He considers all He has predestined you for. He is ready to release the Holy Spirit within you as you open your firewalls He is ready to release all that he has for you as you seek Him. Are you ready for Him?*

... to appear suddenly; become visible, audible, evident, etc., all at once: *I remember the first time I really experienced this fully. I was standing in an airport waiting to return home and there God was speaking to me as if He was standing next to me. I remember smiling so big I thought people around me would think I was crazy. I just stood there hearing God speak, chatting like old friends, keeping me company during my wait. He burst upon the scene and asked me to write this book for Him. I said ok and as we got on the plane I sat down and immediately began to write as fast as I possibly could. It was sudden, it was audible to me and His hand upon my life was evident. What if my capacity to consume would not have been increased, what if I didn't have my TCP Port open at that time, what if I didn't have "burstable" bandwidth to receive such a large download? I would have missed God and this book is about you and me never missing God again!*

So how do we widen the opening and increase the bandwidth and increase our capacity to consume so we are ready for these "bursts" from God?

> *"I pray also that the eyes of your heart maybe enlightened in order that you may know the hope to which he has called you, the riches of his glorious inheritance in the saints, and his incomparably great power for us who believe."* - Ephesians 1:18

The eyes of our heart need to be enlightened so that we might know what He has called us to. This will lead to our understanding of His love for us which widens the tunnel through our increased faith and belief.

As our faith and belief increases, God can reveal more of His mysteries to us because we will have the capacity to understand what He is revealing.

Walking it Out

As I read this chapter I see the wonder of God so clearly and so evident.

God has been increasing my bandwidth and I have been experiencing the bursts I talk about in this chapter.

This chapter is one such burst!

When I originally wrote this I was thinking about bandwidth and God and the wider tunnel but it was a burst from the Holy Spirit that took me on this deeper trail of types of bandwidth and brought me into yet another level of God's mercy and grace.

God continues to enlighten my eyes of understanding as I write this book and continues to amaze and surprise me at His cleverness and His sense of humor.

As I was writing this chapter, God and I were having a great time, sorting through the idea of the bursts, what those look like and how those happen. I was laughing aloud as I wrote this chapter because I was so amazed at God's creativity and so tickled with what He was showing me.

I have come to realize that the bursts don't usually come when we are asking for them or praying about things in particular.

The bursts come when you least expect them but they come because of our faithfulness to spend time before God.

I walk daily in expectation of the wonders of God that will manifest that day. I awake in the morning excited to see what God has planned and what He will be doing in my life as I center myself in Him.

As we begin to open our God port and flow in the things of God, we have to adjust our expectations to His.

I have had to learn to walk in this expectant state and allow God in His timing to speak to me, to bring revelation and to send "bursts" of His love, His thoughts and His knowledge to me as I need it.

I have also found that my feelings can quickly derail me if I am not careful. If we base our spiritual walk on our human emotions we can become discouraged and disappointed.

Our emotions are just that, emotions, they don't make God less of who He is and they don't make us less of who we are in Him. See God is God, the same yesterday, today and forever, unchanging. But, our emotions are a whole other animal and as part of our capacity expansion we have to learn not to let our emotions drive our connection or lack there of to the God port.

We must be aware of our emotions so we can "check them at the door" so to speak in order to access the God port regardless of how we feel! Let me give you an example. I was in my morning quiet time with the Lord and I didn't "feel" like He was there. I was tired and frustrated and wanted to give up. I was wondering why I was even bothering to get up when God wasn't bothering to show up.

As I finished this thought, I realized my emotions were in control instead of my heart for the Lord. I wasn't walking in joy, peace and righteousness but rather fatigue, despair and self pity.

Time to change my state and step into the joy of the Lord! I put on some worship music, sang praises to the Lord and altered my state and presto I could feel the presence of the Lord. We have to remember it's not about "feelings" it's about truth and the truth of His word.

He is always with us; He will never leave us nor forsake us.

We must rest in these promises at all times regardless of how we feel. As we press through chaos, grief and frustration we expand our capacity for the things of God. When we can learn to operate out of what we know to be true, what we know about God and His word regardless of how we feel we can achieve all He has called us to. I say this to encourage you to go deeper with God, open your God port using TCP and begin to experience His true wonder and you too will receive bursts from God that will truly amaze you.

Give it time.

This didn't happen overnight, but rest assured as you are faithful in seeking to open or widen the God port, God will be faithful in meeting you there!

Action Items

Reflect: What kind of communication have you been conducting with God, is it mostly one way? What do your prayers to God sound like, are they mostly requests of what you need?

Do you wait quietly to hear back from God and hear what He is saying? Have you ever experienced a "burst" from God?

What was it like? What were you doing when it happened?

_____
_____
_____
_____
_____
_____
_____
_____

Pray: *Lord thank you that you love us so much that you communication with us through The God Port. Thank you for your word that says Call to Me and I will answer you! Lord help this reader hear your answers open up their two-way communication and teach them to be still and hear your voice. Lord expand this readers capacity to consume the things of You, Your joy, Your peace, Your mighty power and love.*

Continue this prayer with your own words to God, *Lord help me to hear your voice, your answers as you promise them in your word, Lord help me to ....*

Do: Write down a simple new prayer that is focused on seeking God, not the usual I want, I need prayer but something you really desire to know from God.

Whether it's as simple as Lord reveal yourself to me in a more personal way or Lord show me your heart for the lost or Lord show me who I am in you.

Write it down from your heart. God is pricking your heart at this moment for the things of Him he wants to show you, what is He saying?

New Prayer:

_____
_____
_____
_____
_____
_____
_____
_____
_____
_____
_____
_____
_____

Write: Write out your thoughts below. What was God showing you and speaking to you? Just start writing and allow the Holy Spirit to flow through you. One word, one sentence, one paragraph whatever comes to mind.

Chapter Three

"Encryption and Decryption"
What is it and how does it work?

Before we head down this next path let's briefly review what we have learned in the previous two chapters to make sure we are all in sync for this next lesson!

In the first chapter we talked about the idea of ports and firewalls and how that relates to "opening" our communications with God. We learned that God's port number is 3303.

In the last chapter we talked about protocols and bandwidth and how that relates to what type of communication we use with God and how much we can send and/or receive as well as consume.

Lastly we discussed the difference between "fixed" bandwidth that "caps" the amount of information that can be sent and received and "burstable" bandwidth which allows the tunnel to widen as more information is requested and consumed so you don't lose anything being sent!

So now, we have our God port open providing two-way communication at whatever rate God wants to "burst" it to (accessing Port 3303 via TCP).

This is a great start but we have to consider the format in which this information is sent and received.

Let's simplify this with an analogy everyone can understand.

Let's say you are going to a website to do some shopping. You will probably look around and review some of the products on the site to determine what you want to buy.

The owner of the website wants you to be able to understand that information so you will be encouraged to buy their products.

So, the information is simple and informative so that anyone that comes to the website can understand it.

Once you have made your purchase decision and added your product to the shopping cart you are ready to check out.

Now it is time for you to provide some private information to the website so you can purchase the item. This is not information you want everyone to have access to nor does the website owner. They understand your need for security and privacy when entering your personal information; name, address and credit card number and their responsibility to protect your information so others don't "intercept" it.

So how does this happen?

You are still on the same website, you are still accessing the information the same way so what keeps some of the information public and open and some of it private and secure?

The method in which the information is accessed and passed determines whether it is secure or unsecure i.e. public or private. The standard methods for this are Hypertext Transfer Protocol (http) and Hypertext Transfer Protocol Secure (https).

Aren't you glad to finally know what *those* two terms mean!

So, back to our shopping cart example, most of you are probably aware to look for the "lock" icon in your web browser when getting to credit card input pages but have you looked at the address line?

It has now changed from *http* to *https*, which is what causes the lock to appear and tells you the information you are about to enter will be secure when sent. The protocol has changed in real-time to address the security concerns of the user.

This is important to realize because God can change the communication protocol with us as well in order to keep us pressed in and seeking Him.

We will come back to this idea a bit later.

What does the https really mean? How is it secure? It means that once you type your information in and click send the secure protocol invokes a method of encryption to make your information unreadable and therefore your information is locked with a key.

The only one that can read the information is the one with the key to unlock it. This is encryption and decryption.

This passes information through the port unreadable to anyone that might be listening in or intercepting it and then makes it readable again once it passes through the firewall on the other end of the port.

This is referred to as Secure Socket Layers or SSL.

This not only opens an end-to-end connection as with TCP but it opens it up via a secure channel so it can only be read by the "eyes" or "computers" it is intended for.

Encryption is the process of transforming information (plain text) using an algorithm (called cipher) to make it unreadable to anyone except those possessing special knowledge, usually referred to as a key.

Decryption is to make the encrypted information readable again by using the key to the cipher - i.e. to make it unencrypted. (*http://en.wikipedia.org/wiki/Encryption*)

How does this relate to the God Port and communicating with God? Well, why did Jesus speak in parables?

Why do our eyes of our heart need to be enlightened?

Why can we read the same bible verse two different times and get a totally different perspective from it?

Why can a pastor read us a verse on Sunday and totally unravel the mysteries that lay behind it when we didn't get anything out of it at all on our own?

Why could everyone at Pentecost hear the same voice teaching but receive the information in their native language so they could understand it?

That's right encryption and decryption at its best, real time with ciphers and keys, accessible by all of us who believe.

Let's break it down by using the example of the parables in the bible. Jesus took plain information, applied His Kingdom knowledge to it (cipher), changed it (unreadable) and spoke it as a parable, a story. Which means you cannot understand it unless you possess special knowledge i.e. a key.

Do we possess special knowledge as children of God?

Do we have special keys to receive Kingdom knowledge?

> *The disciples came to him and asked, "Why do you speak to the people in parables?" He replied, "The knowledge of the secrets of the kingdom of heaven has been given to you, but not to them.* Matthew 13:10-11

Jesus goes on to say, *"But blessed are your eyes because they see, and your ears because they hear. For I tell you the truth, many prophets and righteous men longed to see what you see but did not see it, and to hear what you hear but did not hear it."* Matthew 13:16-17

Many prophets and righteous men longed to see it but did not?

Isn't this us at times, longing to see the truths of God but we are missing the "key" to decipher it?

We can read a passage in the bible and get nothing from it one day and the next time we read it the passage comes to life! Every word in the verse jumps out at us and brings us understanding and hope. We now have the key to decrypt the message and see how God intended it just for us.

We always had the key but we did not have the capacity to consume the truth that lay behind it.

What do you suppose the cipher is and what is the key in the God Port?

How does God send encrypted information to us and decrypt it when it arrives?

Is it always encrypted, or sometimes is He sending the information for public use?

How does information get from us to God, can we encrypt it if so who decrypt's it?

> "...*Christ Jesus, who died...more than that, who was raised to life...is at the right hand of God and is also interceding for us.*- Romans 8:34
>
> "*My little children, these things write I unto you, that ye sin not. And if any man sin, we have an advocate with the Father, Jesus Christ the righteous.*" 1 John 2:1
>
> "*If you love me, you will obey what I command. And I will ask the Father, and he will give you another Counselor to be with you forever...the Spirit of truth. The world cannot accept him, because it neither sees him nor knows him. But you know him, for he lives with you and will be in you.*" John 14:15-17

I believe for us today that the Counselor Jesus speaks of; the Holy Spirit is the key and the cipher for our God Port.

He decrypts messages from God to us and allows us to encrypt messages (speaking in tongues when we know not what to pray – Romans 8:26) to Jesus as He intercedes on our behalf to the Father.

Jesus as He intercedes on our behalf receives revelation from God and communicates that to us through the Holy Spirit, our Counselor. He reveals (decrypts) the mysteries of God as we are ready and prepared.

God provides lots of information for public use because He wants everyone to come to a saving knowledge of Him. But as we deepen our journey God wants to pour out revelation to us, just for us so we can persevere and accomplish the assignments He has predestined us for.

God passes this information encrypted and allows the Holy Spirit to decrypt it and reveal it to us and counsel us on its meaning and application.

> *"I will give you the keys of the kingdom of heaven; whatever you bind on earth will be bound in heaven, and whatever you loose on earth will be loosed in heaven."* Matthew 16:19

We have the keys to decrypt all God has for us, let's open the God Port, remove the bricks in our firewall, press into the Holy Spirit, increase our capacity for consumption and use our keys to decrypt the messages of God!

Well as all good technology folks do let's diagram this God Port out and see what we have learned.

God →Jesus(God's Firewall) → Holy Spirit→Heart / Mind (Our Firewall)→Us

Once the firewalls are all opened and activated there becomes two way communications throughout the network:

God ←>Jesus(God's Firewall) <→ Holy Spirit(cipher and key)<→ Heart/Mind (Our Firewall)<→Us

Now all the pieces are in place, how do we "activate" them? How do we open the God Port? How do we open our firewall to allow God in? How do we learn two-way communication?

How do we increase our bandwidth to be receiving revelation from God all the time and be prepared for the "bursts" and make sure the information is being decrypted so we can fully understand it and act upon it?

How do we apply this practically in our daily life?

In short, the Holy Spirit enlightens our eyes of understanding as we read God's word to help us "consume" it and make it real and living in our life. The Holy Spirit brings us revelation and understanding in our prayer time, in our worship time and in our quiet time with God as our God Port is opened and expanded.

Simple enough, of course not!

We need to break this down into several key elements (keys to the Kingdom perhaps) and I will spend the next several chapters doing so now that we have the basics outlined.

It's time to roll up our sleeves and begin to understand how to practically apply this God port theory and make it a reality!

Walking it Out

God is so absolutely amazing!

As I was contemplating what to call this chapter and how to relate it to technology and what really needed to be said, God's voice came streaming through the God Port.

He said to talk about encryption and decryption and I thought wow we are in for a wild ride now!

As I began to type God unraveled more of His mysteries to me and invoked the Holy Spirit to decrypt this message to me and receive the revelation God was bringing me.

I was able to receive this revelation because my capacity had been expended by God and I was prepared for the "burst".

I had spent several weeks actually praying and preparing for the weekend I wrote these chapters. God had been teaching me during our time together and preparing me with smaller bursts.

I remember one day after spending my morning time in prayer and reading the word that I had to go to a technology conference for the morning. I was grounded in the word and God for the day and I was ready. As I sat in the conference God began to speak to me about some business ideas and answers to some questions I had been pondering with Him days before.

There it was…the burst, the stream from the God port, simple, clean and clear. I jotted some notes down on paper as God gave me the ideas so I would not forget them, then turned back to the conference speaker to hear what he was saying.

It was a short few-minutes burst, but timely, revelatory and clearly God imparting wisdom and knowledge to me.

The short bursts were practice and rehearsal for the larger bursts to make sure my capacity was expanded and I could stay with the revelation God was imparting to me.

I spent the next two days typing as fast as I could to capture all that God was giving me.

By the time I was done that weekend, my eyes were bloodshot and I think the image of my computer screen was burned into them! I couldn't pull myself away; I didn't want to miss anything God was downloading to me. My husband had to practically pull me away from the computer to go to bed. I was afraid if I went to bed I would lose the connection and miss what God had for me. I had not experienced this level of burst before and I wasn't sure if it would still be there in the morning!

God was expanding my capacity to a whole new level and guess what? I awoke the next morning, went to church and when I got home to start writing the burst continued!

God is faithful and will make sure we get His message if we stay pressed into Him and what He is doing.

Someone told me once that the first voice we usually hear is God and then the very next voice we here is either our carnal man or the enemy trying to talk us out of what God just so clearly spoke to us!

Reason enters on the scene and faith walks out. The fear and doubt and disbelief creep in and we don't act on what God said.

One moment it is so clear the next moment we are questioning everything we just heard. But as we continue to learn how to open the God port and keep the connection open we begin to believe what we hear is from God.

Action Items

Reflect: Are there bible versus that God has directed you to but you do not understand? Are you drawn to certain scriptures but don't fully understand them? Have you asked God to enlighten your eyes with understanding?

Do you remember a time reading a scripture and it coming to life? How did that feel, what were you doing differently during that bible reading than other times?

_____
_____
_____
_____
_____
_____
_____
_____
_____
_____
_____
_____

Pray: *Lord thank you for this readers desire to have your word decrypted to them, to have your mysteries revealed and to bring understanding, wisdom and knowledge to them. Lord allow your Holy Spirit within this reader to be ignited and begin decrypting the things of You. Bring fresh revelation even at this minute Lord to encourage this reader and lift their spirit and sense the Holy Spirit within them. Jesus thank you for interceding at all times on their behalf.*

Continue this prayer with your own words to God, *Lord enlighten my eyes, reveal your mysteries to me, bring me revelation and understanding of the things of you as I press in to who you are.*

Do: Write down one bible verse or section of scripture you want to pursue the deeper meaning of with God. Is there a verse He is bringing to mind? Write this one down and then read it and let the word marinate in your spirit as you seek the Holy Spirit to decrypt it for you. If you don't know of a verse or scripture consider Ephesians Chapter 1 for a starting point.

Study Verse:

_____
_____
_____
_____
_____

Write: Write out your thoughts below. What was God showing you and speaking to you? Just start writing and allow the Holy Spirit to flow through you. One word, one sentence, one paragraph whatever comes to mind.

_____
_____
_____
_____
_____
_____
_____
_____
_____
_____
_____
_____
_____
_____
_____
_____

Chapter Four

Pings and Trace Routes – Pursuing the God Port

Now that we know what the God Port is we need to talk about the effort it will take to get there.

Understanding this idea of pursuing God is critical to the next several chapters as we learn the keys to opening the God port. The keys won't work if they are not used correctly, i.e. if our hearts are not in the right place.

Remember God knows your heart, but do you?

Pings and trace routes are actions used to send out signals across the internet to search for a particular connection.

A *ping* determines whether a host computer is reachable or not across the internet. It can also determine the round trip time it takes to get a response back from the host computer and records any packet loss during the process.

A *trace route* is a bit different in that it determines the route taken to reach the requested destination.

This was how I was searching for God; I was sending out a ping and waiting for a response back from Him telling me He was there but my routes taken were not always successful and I often felt my prayers were falling on "deaf" ears.

Keep in mind you only send out a ping when you are not sure the connection is open and working, you only send a trace route when it appears things are taking too long to get to their destination so you want to see what route they are taking. These are troubleshooting methods to determine if there is a problem and where it lies.

Do we only communicate with God when we are in troubleshooting mode?

Be honest!

If the bulk of our communications with God are pings and trace routes, searching for Him, trying to find Him, hoping He is out there then how effective do you think these really are? This is where I was and where I was starting from and once I began to realize I needed to get out of troubleshooting mode and into a deeper, consistent, seeking mode, I began to explore this verse and what it really meant.

> *"You will seek me and find me when you **seek me** with **all your heart**. Jeremiah 29:13*

You might say, but I have done this, I am seeking Him but He's not there, He's not answering, He's not listening, I can't find Him! He is there, He is always listening and He is sharing His heart with us but the noise of the world is winning out.

Notice the first part of that verse says "seek" me. What does that mean, how do we seek Him?

I had to apply my "key" to this and really begin to understand what it means; here is the decryption the Holy Spirit provided me.

Seek means to go in search or quest of…have you searched for God, quested for Him and the answers you are looking for?

Another term for seek is to pursue or follow.

I believe God is calling us to "pursue" Him with all our hearts. Let's look at the definitions of pursue to really uncover what God is asking of us.

While follow implies simply to go after, pursue has a deeper meaning and objective. Pursue means to follow with earnestness and a view, to attain some definite objective.

I believe this is the type of seeking God is asking us to do of Him. God wants us to seek Him with earnestness and to attain the objective of finding Him and not just finding Him (pinging Him) but discovering Him.

Discover means to gain sight or knowledge of, this implies a greater activity on our part than just finding. The pursuit doesn't end when you find Him, it only just begins unlike a ping which ends when the end connection is found.

Another meaning of pursue is to go in search of or hunt for! I love this one, when was the last time you truly searched God out or actually hunted for Him?

Hunting implies pursuing with force, strength, energy, power and intensity. Do you see the difference, are you beginning to understand the depth of this verse and what it means to "seek" God.

It's time to stop pinging Him and sending out trace routes and it's time to truly start seeking Him.

Pursue can also mean to occupy oneself with, isn't this one great. Can you imagine occupying yourself with God?

This is the type of activity, pursuit we are talking about with the God Port, occupying ourselves with His voice, His revelation and His word all day. Let's stay with this a bit longer, pursue also means to move behind in the same path or direction of, hence go with.

Our objective of connecting with God through the God Port and hearing His voice is for the purpose of being able to go with Him, to follow in His same path.

Jesus only did what He saw the Father doing, isn't that our goal as well?

How can we accomplish this if we aren't on the same path so we can go with God?

The other meaning of pursue is to copy after, to take example of. Wasn't Christ our example of the Father, are we not to copy Him and become like him?

Pursue means to accept as authority, to adopt opinions of, to obey and to yield. This calls us to yield to God, adopt His opinions and obey Him. Pursue also means to understand the meaning, connection or force of; do we understand the true force of God?

I am just beginning to get a glimpse of this.

The last two meanings of pursue are my favorite.

Pursue also means to watch, keep eyes fixed upon while in motion, keep mind upon while in progress, to keep up with. It also means to walk in, as a road or a cause, to attend upon closely as a profession or calling.

Wow, these two really hit the objectives of the God Port head on and this was my heart when I began this journey.

When you are connected to the God Port all day every day you are attending to God and you have your eyes fixed upon Him while you are in motion for the day and He is in motion, you are keeping up with Him!

He becomes your cause, your profession, and your calling. Notice it says you are attending to God; He is not attending to you. I believe we get this mixed up at times.

We think it is God's job to attend to us but it is not we are to attend to Him first then all things will be added!

Remember now this is all part of the original scripture of "seek" him with all your heart. Do you have a bigger picture now of what that means, can you still say you are doing this?

I certainly couldn't. As I began to understand this I realized how inadequate my prior attempts had been and that my pursuit of Him was little more than a few pings and trace routes sent out on occasion during troubled times.

There is one more verse I have to cover while we have the deeper meaning of seek and pursue in our minds.

> *"But seek ye first the kingdom of God, and his righteousness; and all these things shall be added unto you."* Matthew 6:33

Again keep in mind the idea of seek, pursue, attend to the Kingdom of God when – first!

Then what, all these things will be given to you as well.

What things are those you ask? The things we all worry about that God tells us not to!

> *"And why do you worry about clothes? See how the lilies of the field grow. They do not labor or spin. Yet I tell you that not even Solomon in all his splendor was dressed like one of these. If that is how God clothes the grass of the field, which is here today and tomorrow is thrown into the fire, will he not much more clothe you. O you of little faith? So do not worry, saying 'What shall we eat?' or 'What shall we drink?' or ' What shall we wear?' For the pagans run after all these things, and your heavenly Father knows that you need them."* Matthew 6:28-32

So now you have it the full picture we are to "seek the Kingdom of God" and we are to "seek God with all our heart".

We now understand the depth of what that really means and remember the verse started out saying, "you will seek me and find me when you seek me with all your heart" so will it happen outside of this?

No, you must seek Him with all your heart.

There is no other way. Yes you guessed it I want to traverse down the path of what "all" your heart means just to wrap this up.

All means the whole of, the greatest possible, every and nothing but.

Well, there are hundreds of iterations we can derive from this but let's review a few that the Holy Spirit revealed to me. This was God speaking directly to me so I am restating it in His words because He is speaking it to you as well.

"Attend to me with the greatest possible heart."

"Keep your eyes fixed upon me, while in motion with the whole of your heart."

"Occupy yourself with me with nothing but your heart."

There is so much more depth in there, I think we will need another book just for pursuing God!

So now that we understand what it means to pursue God and what it takes to open the God Port, why don't we do it? Is it laziness, too busy, other priorities, not important enough, won't produce results, isn't your "cup of tea"?

I think it is because we don't truly believe in the power that God has promised us in His word and His word in general.

Have you read it, really read it?

> *"That power is like the working of his mighty strength, which he exerted in Christ when he raised him from the dead and seated him at his right hand in the heavenly realms, far above all rule and authority, power and dominion, and every title that can be given, not only in the present age but also in the one to come."* Ephesians 1:19-21

The power that raised Christ from the dead is the same power that has been given to us through the Holy Spirit.

Read it…it's in God's word.

Oh wait - do we truly believe in God's word?

That it's true and real and the living word of God? God breathed and inspired?

Well if we don't truly believe in God's word and we don't truly believe in God's power…then why should we spend time with Him?

The Truth Project taught by Focus on the Family and Dale Tackett challenges us with this question: "Do we really believe what we really believe is really real?"

Let's ponder this for a moment, if we believe the bible is God inspired and His living word for us, if we really believe this and that His word is true then why don't we live in the power and might of His word?

Is it because we don't really believe it deep in our hearts, that we don't really believe it is real?

Did Jesus heal the sick?

Yes.

Did Jesus raise the dead?

Yes.

Did Jesus perform signs and miracles?

Yes.

Did God raise Jesus from the dead?

Yes!

Does the verse above say that we have that same power that raised Christ from the dead?

Yes!

Are we moving and acting in this power?

No!

Why?

I say disbelief, disbelief that God's word is for us for today and that God has placed us here for a "time such as this." Disbelief that His word is true and that we can move in His power and might in all that we say and do.

How do we overcome this disbelief? By seeking Him with all our heart in the manner we uncovered above.

Not just one of the ways we can pursue but all of them; with zeal, with force and with the tenacity of nothing but our hearts. We must take time to press into God and the things of God so that we can truly put on the full characteristics of Christ who only did what He saw His Father doing.

How do we do this, how do we begin this pursuit?

Well, I began it the only way I knew how, by hanging out with those that had already achieved this!

In business we know that we need mentors and coaches, we know that if we want to achieve something to look for others that have been successful in those areas and learn from them. I applied this same thought process to seeking God. I began attending conferences where I knew God was showing up, I began pursuing God where He was and I began spending time with those that were obviously spending time with God.

You can tell by talking to someone or just looking at them that they are spending time with God, they wear His glory; they exude His strength and confidence and His humility and grace.

You see I had stopped hearing that "still small voice," God was changing His protocol for speaking to me and I had to adapt.

So, I went in search of God and I began to hunt Him, to pursue Him with zeal and a perseverance I had not had before. And, God was faithful, He met me there and He began to speak to me and show me things through others.

He directed me to books I needed to read on hearing His voice, He directed me to prayer teams that prayed for me, and He directed me to Pastors, business people and other people that truly knew Him. Then He directed me to a wonderful young lady that said this to me: "Spend more time with God and He will show you all that you are asking of Him."

My world stopped, my heart sank, and my mind raced.

How did she know I wasn't?

I was mad at first, how dare her, then I was convicted and began rehearsing those firewall bricks, you know the ones, guilt and shame! Then the grace of God came upon me and He said He would meet me there, in that time with Him and show me all I had been asking.

I knelt down and prayed right then and decided it was time, really time, to give God my time.

The next several chapters are my journey on how I spent that time with God, how I learned to press in and how I learned to open my God port and realize I did have the keys to the Kingdom and just needed to use them!

Walking it Out

Pursuing God was not an easy task and it took time and continues to take time.

It also took perseverance in those early morning hours when I didn't feel like getting up, when I didn't feel God's presence, when I didn't receive instant answers to prayers and revelation but I pressed on anyway. I pressed on because I believed God's word to be true.

I didn't have a lot else to go on but His word so I persevered. I spent countless early morning hours seeking Him and learning what that really meant and how to do it.

God wants us to pursue Him, to set everything else aside and seek His presence and His very being.

God is waiting for us, waiting to deliver to us what He has called us to.

God is looking to and fro for those that are chasing after Him, searching for Him, hunting Him down.

As we seek Him and draw near to Him, He draws us to Him; He becomes our gravity to pull us into His Kingdom, into His presence and allows us to bring His Kingdom to earth!

We have to learn to "contend" for the things of God and the promises He has made to us. Those visions He has given you regarding your purpose, contend for them. Your children seeking the Lord and desiring His will for their lives contend for their purposes, contend for their salvation and their transformation.

Do you have a spouse that is not saved or not walking in the things of God…contend for them!

Are you building a kingdom business and desire profits and sustainability…contend for it!

Somewhere in the process of being saved some of us got the impression everything is easy after that. I know I did and when things didn't go perfectly there I was asking God, where was He, why was He allowing this to happen or why I was not seeing what He promised. Pursuing God is contending for the things of God and His plan and purpose for your life.

We only fail if we give up, stay pressed in, keep pursuing and press in toward the goal for which you have been called.

Action Items

Reflect: Do you only communicate with God when you are in troubleshooting mode? Have you pursued God with your whole heart? What have past attempts at pursuing God looked like and what happened?

What caused you to get off track or abandon the pursuit?

_____
_____
_____
_____
_____
_____
_____
_____
_____

Pray: *Lord, thank you for the power that is within us, thank you for leaving your Holy Spirit with us so we would not be without you here on earth. Lord as this reader focuses in on how to begin their pursuit again and continue it until your kingdom comes, give them revelation and vision on what that will look like for them. Lord show them your power and the truth of your word so they will be encouraged to stay on the journey, always pressing in, always persevering, never giving up the pursuit. Lord come alongside this reader as they learn how to "hunt You down" with their whole heart.*

Continue this prayer with your own words to God, *Lord show me who I am in you, show me the truth of your word, expand my belief that I might press into this journey with you. God of the universe, You are mighty and I…*

Do: Review the pursuing God statements in this chapter, which one resonates with you? Write down the one that inspires you the most, which gives you a vision of pursuit that you can focus on each day and run after with God. Feel free to write your own as God lays it on your heart.

Define your pursuit of God:

_____
_____
_____
_____
_____

Write: Write out your thoughts below. What was God showing you and speaking to you? Just start writing and allow the Holy Spirit to flow through you. One word, one sentence, one paragraph whatever comes to mind.

_____
_____
_____
_____
_____
_____
_____
_____
_____
_____
_____
_____
_____
_____

Chapter Five

Uploads and Downloads – How do we open the connection to the God Port?

Let's think about when we feel closest to God.

Is it during worship time at church, during your prayer time or when you are reading His word?

Is it while you are singing along to your favorite praise song on the radio?

Or maybe it is when you are watching the sunrise and appreciating the Glory of all God's creation?

It is these actions that initiate the open port to God. The open port is the gateway to stepping into His presence.

What brings you into the presence of God?

What opens our port to God is different for everyone because we are "uniquely made" so don't get hung up in how others do it but rather search out with God the things that draw you near to Him, that bring you into His presence and bring His praises on your lips. Work with God to learn how to call Him according to your DNA and His unique relationship with you.

I will offer a few tips and starting points but remain pliable to what God begins to do as you "call Him" and make this journey your own.

The term upload and download is used to reference files, or data, or requests that are being "passed" from a local computer to a remote server and vice versa.

This is happening constantly when you are "surfing" the web.

When you go to a web page you send a request to the remote server and ask to see the "home" page of a website for example. The remote server receives the request, considers it, interprets it, and prepares the information you requested, interprets it back, and sends back the information or page you requested.

Now there are a lot of other things going on during this request and many of the terms we have discussed in prior chapters are being "invoked" to make this happen but for this chapter we are going to keep it simple and just talk about the movement of data, and how it relates to opening the God port.

The reason the remote server needs an interpreter is that the requests can come in many formats and languages(html, asp, php, java and much more) but the server can only receive information one way, in 0 and 1's, bits and bytes, machine code!

No matter where the request originates it always ends up in 0 and 1's for the server to understand it, formulate a response and prepare to send it back.

Now get this - before it can send it back, it has to send it back through the interpreter to translate it back into the original language it arrived in so the local computer can read it again.

The interpreter becomes the gatekeeper of the information and if it can't understand the request, it will send back an error message.

If it can understand the request, it will interpret it, send to server, await the response, interpret it and send it back. The interpreters are very fast and very smart and can take a "malformed" request that would normally cause the server to return an error and "reformat" it on the fly according to certain rules as it interprets it and send it on to the server so it can be processed successfully.

When we pray to God we are "uploading" information to Him.

Prayers are in the form of "requests" most of the time, Lord help me feel better, Lord cover my financial needs, Lord help me get this new job, Lord you want me to buy this car, right?

Lord should I, could I, would you!

God receives those requests via His interpreter Jesus Christ considers them and then downloads the response back down.

So, we are the local computer and God in Heaven is the remote server. The word says that Jesus is forever interceding to the Father on our behalf so that would make Jesus the interpreter.

Jesus receives our prayer requests as we speak them, He "interprets" them according to what He knows is best for us (reformatting on the fly), speaks them to the Father and then receives them back according to what He hears the Father saying, interprets them again so He can "download" God's response back to us so we can understand it.

Did you see that?

Jesus is our interpreter and only wants what is best for us from the Father. He is standing in the gap 24 hours a day to receive our requests, reformat them if needed and interpret them and send them on to the Father.

Why does He reformat them you are thinking?

Well do you think everything we pray for is what is best for us as we begin our journey?

Do you think Jesus is going to intercede for us to the Father for things He knows will be bad for us?

I don't think so.

Jesus knows the plans the Lord has for us, Jesus knows what we are predestined for and Jesus knows according to all He sees the Father doing what we need at any given time and especially those times when we don't know ourselves!

Let's get an example out here so we can try to wrap our minds around this. I might pray something like this:

Dear Jesus please help me get this new job. Jesus knows God has placed me in my current job for a reason and a season and that time is not up yet.

So, Jesus might interpret my prayer to the Father as: Dear God send your grace and wisdom to Wende and direct her to Sally to be encouraged so she can stay and complete the work you have assigned her to.

God says absolutely, and Jesus sends back to me: Wende, be patient, stay the course and when it's time a new job will open up and while you are waiting why don't you start a bible study with Sally.

Now, this is a really simple example, and I realize our prayers can be complex and our situations and circumstances can be overwhelming. Still, all the more reason to rejoice in the fact that Jesus is advocating to the Father on our behalf according to what is best for us until our prayers begin to reflect the Father's will for our lives!

This is a huge shift in how we pray and what we pray. This is one of the conduits for opening the port and breaking down the firewalls.

The other aspect of uploads and downloads is praise and worship time, which is the other conduit to opening the God port.

We talked about the firewall, the brick wall that needs to be opened. How do we punch through the wall between us and God, what is that firewall and how do we "breach" it?

What is the first step?

Praise and worship is a great catalyst for breaching those bricks in the firewall and punching through to God.

There is another aspect of this, that God showed me.

When we sing a praise song to God, it's already in His language, the angels' language and all of Heaven; Jesus is not needed to interpret but is there to increase the power of our praise, to escalate it to the Father's ear.

See praise and worship doesn't need interpreted because God inhabits the praises of His people. The angels sing praise songs and worship God the Father and the Son all day long through all eternity.

All of heaven knows the sound of praise and worship and joins in as we sing to bring Glory and Honor to God.

During our praise and worship, Jesus is still interceding as the mercy and grace of God descends from Heaven and falls on the room for us to experience a piece of Heaven and a glimpse of God and His glory.

This is why we spend time in prayer and worship, seeking the Father and yearning for His presence and thereby opening the God Port!

> *"But thou art holy O thou that inhabitest the praises of Israel."* Psalm 22:3.

In other words, God inhabits the praises of His people so this is a good place to start especially if you are new at this like I was.

It brings familiarity and grounding to get comfortable with calling God. Starting with praise and worship invites God into what you are embarking on, you may find that you will spend much of your time here for awhile.

Accessing the God Port will change over time and get easier as you get comfortable with keeping the port open and receiving ongoing streams of information from God.

The idea is to eventually be able to keep the God Port open and just "tune in" to it as directed by God to receive revelation and understanding as He streams it to you.

Understand that this takes practice and time to figure out what works for you.

> *"I praise you because I am fearfully and wonderfully made; your works are wonderful, I know that full well."* Psalm 139:14

This verse is critical because if we don't believe this statement if we don't begin to see the wonder of this verse we won't see the wonder of God in us.

We are fearfully and wonderfully made and God adores us!

> *"Indeed, the very hairs on your head are all numbered. Do not fear; you are more valuable than many sparrows.* Luke 12:7

It doesn't say some of the hairs are numbered, it says all of the hairs on your head are numbered by God. He is a God who cares about details, the very details of your life, and the very hairs on your head.

> *"Therefore I will praise you, O Lord, among the nations; I will sing praises to your name."* 2 Samuel 22:50

David as we know was a man after God's own heart; let's see how important he thinks praising God is.

> *"Four thousand are to be gatekeepers and four thousand are to praise the LORD with the musical instruments I have provided for that purpose."* I Chronicles 23:5

I love our churches praise and worship time because it opens my God Port every time. I know I am in His presence and I have had an encounter with Him. Still, I wanted more of this than just Sunday at church, so short of having the worship teams follow me around I decided I better figure out how to enter into His presence on my own.

So, after I failed miserably at my first few attempts at "quiet time" with God as you will read later, I turned to what I knew, praise and worship.

This was something I knew how to do and could be successful at it so this is where I started as I began to spend more time with God. I began to conduct my own praise and worship sessions every morning. I pulled out my praise and worship cd's for backup and began to sing unto the Lord.

This was the start of my quiet time with God, not so quiet but very productive. As I sang and worshipped the Lord, there in my office, all by myself, guess who joined me?

Yes, He did.

Believe me, spending time with God if you have never really done it is a learning experience. I had to move out of the anxiety and worries of getting something accomplished and really begin just spending time with Him.

Being in His presence just to be there and not wanting anything in return and learning to enjoy His companionship, His friendship, His presence without feeling like I needed to be doing something.

Being a type 'A' personality this was extremely hard for me.

I began my mornings listening to worship music, singing along and settling my mind onto the things of God. Some mornings this was all I did and it brought me the joy and peace of the Lord.

Other mornings I would move into prayer and supplication.

Thanking the Lord for His grace and mercy, thanking Him for all He had done for me and all He had provided and of course at some point the prayers would move to what I needed from Him.

Sometimes, the Lord would bring certain friends, relatives, clients or staff members to mind and I would lift them in prayer.

Sometimes He would bring situations to mind that He wanted me to pray for. I cherish and honor this time of prayer and interceding and sometimes will find myself spending most of my morning in this activity.

I began to notice as I spent more time in praise and worship my prayers shifted from Lord I need, Lord please help to Lord show me more of you, Lord show me your heart.

My prayers became less about me and what I needed and more about Him and who He is. I wanted more of Him, I wanted to understand Him and know Him better.

What makes Him leap for joy and cry rivers of tears, what keeps Him awake at night instead of what keeps me awake at night! My prayers were moving from the one way protocol to the two way protocol and I was beginning to receive back from God. About the time I realized this I got very excited and wanted to receive revelation from Him every morning at that very moment.

But guess what…as I began expecting back from God at that moment the port would shut back down! What was I doing wrong?

I realized later that I needed to just focus on the prayer, praise and worship and pressing into God and that the revelation would come later.

I remember the first time I experienced this, I was sitting in a meeting late morning and all of a sudden I received a burst from God, a download of answers and next steps for my business. I wasn't asking Him for it at that time but here it came, wow!

You see, earlier that morning I had spent time with God in prayer and worship, just enjoying our time together with no expectations of return. I finished our time and went off to my meetings for the day and the revelation began to come and continued to flow throughout the day.

I was experiencing the fullness of the God Port and what it really meant, it was a monumental day and monumental shift in my understanding God and I wanted more!

I was now tuning into God's heart and seeking His face and in return He was showing me who He was.

I have to say the journey has been incredible and I still feel like it has just begun and yet I have come so far, but now I can see how much more God is when we let Him out of our little box and begin to allow Him to really move in our lives.

Walking it Out

This transition did not happen overnight and my awareness of how I prayed and how they shifted has only been of late.

It's only after we spend a significant amount of time with God that we begin to truly experience the renewing of our mind, we begin to experience life according to God's purposes not our own.

As you spend more time with God you will want to spend more time with God and it will go from being a chore to being a joy. You will begin to walk in and reflect the joy, peace and righteousness of God and people will notice which gives you a chance to fulfill the great commission, go into all the world and make disciples of men. Keep in mind, God knows our heart and in prayer and worship time He often reveals what He knows back to us and it's not always pretty!

Praise and worship opens our heart to God and exposes who we are to ourselves. The funny part is God already knows all that stuff and we think we have been keeping some big secret from Him. We can either face it head on, receive the lessons He is trying to teach us or we can step out of His presence, stuff those things back down and leave them for another day.

Trust me when I say there will be another day.

As you press into the Lord in praise and worship let yourself be vulnerable and enter into the joy and happiness of His presence. Become transparent before God and you will become transparent before man.

As you open the God port and really truly plug in to God's word, the Holy Spirit within you and God's love for you, you will be forever changed.

As we stop "striving" to be good and start "seeking" the Lord we move from walking out our salvation to bringing His kingdom to earth and walking as citizens of the King!

Action Items

Reflect: When was the last time you just worshipped and praised God without an ulterior motive or selfish agenda?

Have you spent time with God just to spend time with Him?

How much time do you spend with God outside of activities like church, bible studies, etc…? Think about a time you felt close to God, you felt connected and your God Port was open, what were you doing?

_____
_____
_____
_____
_____
_____

Pray: *Oh Lord our Lord how majestic is your name in all the earth! Lord rise up worship songs in this readers heart, bring music to their ears and release the worshipper inside of them.*

Lord thank you that you inhabit the praises of your people inhabit this readers praises now as they worship and praise you. Fill their heart to overflowing with your love and compassion that they might truly know they are in Your presence. Fill the room they are in with your presence, surround them with your angels and move Your Holy Spirit with in them that they would know they have encountered You this day!

Continue this prayer with your own words to God, *Lord teach me to praise and worship you, to seek you with all of my heart and to set everything aside to just spend time with you. Lord inhabit my praises receive my worship as a living sacrifice and bring me into your presence. Lord* ………………………………..

Do: Write down a thank you statement to God. Thanking God is praising God, search your heart, listen to what God is speaking to you and pour out your thanks to the Lord.

Thank you God:

_____
_____
_____
_____
_____
_____
_____
_____

Write: Write out your thoughts below. What was God showing you and speaking to you? Just start writing and allow the Holy Spirit to flow through you. One word, one sentence, one paragraph whatever comes to mind.

_____
_____
_____
_____
_____
_____
_____
_____
_____
_____
_____
_____
_____
_____

Chapter Six

Search Engines and Keywords – How do we learn about God and gain new insights?

We learned in the prior chapter that to open the God port we needed to spend time with Him in prayer and worship.

The second objective is to increase the bandwidth and get on the right protocol, so how is this accomplished?

We must spend time in God's word.

Why is this important?

How does this help open the port and get us connected?

Well let's go to technology. If we are looking for something on the internet we search for it using Google, Yahoo, Bing or other search engines.

We go to the search engines because they have indexed much of the information on the web and therefore make it easier to find what we are looking for. Their little "spiders" as they call them are sent out to "crawl" the internet day and night looking for new sites, new content, and new products.

When they find stuff, they bring the "food" back to the source and catalog it in their search engine according to keywords for easy retrieval by users.

So now, instead of us having to look at every single website we can go to a single website, type in a keyword and search for what we are looking for.

Why do we search the web, what are we looking for?

Answers! Solutions to a problem, etc...

We search the web because we are looking for someone that has already figured out the answer to our problem; they already have a solution and we want to use it and have them help us with our problem. Now, keep in mind when we put in keywords we receive many responses back, many options and lots of different paths to follow and determine where the best solution is, or who the best person is for the job.

The search engines job is not to identify the best plumber only all the plumbers that they can find and then we have to decide based on gathering more information which plumber to choose for the job.

What is our search engine for God and how does this help us connect to the God Port?

The obvious answer is The Bible - it's cataloged by Old and New Testament, Books of the Bible and chapters and verses.

If we have some type of study bible then we can usually access additional classifications by characters of the bible, words, phrases, periods in time, themes and more, i.e. keywords. So when we go to the bible to find an answer is it as easy as finding a plumber on the web?

Our search for answers from God takes more time because we don't know where to find them. The Bible is filled with parables and stories, commandments, who begat who, praises, lamentations, prophetic words and letters. Where do we start, how do we find what we are looking for?

We need a search engine to improve this process, to point us in the right direction so we can quickly and easily access the right scripture to unravel the answers from God regarding our request.

So, while searching for a plumber on the internet search engine is pretty simple, our search for God and His answers takes more dedication, more time, more effort and attention.

Let me present a deeper idea here - what if we build an internal search engine to God?

What if we spent enough time in God's word that it became in grained in our very being?

What if we could feed ourselves keywords and receive back instantaneously the scripture and the principles of God that applies to it?

I am not suggesting we stop reading God's word I am suggesting we never stop reading God's word!

Remember who is our cipher and key, the Holy Spirit.

So, as the word of God becomes a part of us, our head knowledge and our heart knowledge then the Holy Spirit can receive our keywords and instantaneously return back the answers we are looking for according to God's word.

Now we have an instant list of scriptures and verses from the Holy Spirit to go to in the Bible. The Holy Spirit uses what you know in God's word, specific verse you have read and returns them to you when you need them to meet the specific request you are searching for answers to. You go to God's word; the Holy Spirit enlightens your eyes to understanding at that moment for that answer you were seeking.

> *"Thy Word is a lamp unto my feet, and a light unto my path."* Psalm 119:105

So how do we increase our bandwidth, by reading the Word of God!

As we dwell in God's word, we begin to understand Him better and begin to see His heart for us and His love for us.

Remember we talked about capacity versus consumption when we discussed bandwidth. We have to increase our capacity to be able to consume God's direction for our lives.

We increase our capacity by reading God's word, by understanding who He is and who we are in Christ. God has called us each to this place for a time such as this and, as He raises up His body of believers, His word will be spread to all nations and heaven will be established here on earth.

God loves all of man and is jealous for every soul so He is giving us time to make sure everyone has heard His word.

If His word is so important that He wants everyone to hear it don't you suppose we should begin to read it, hear it, absorb it and consume it and let the Holy Spirit become our search engine to God?

Until we really believe what we really believe is really real we won't be successful at giving up our time to God.

There you have it…there is the answer; there is the root of the problem, why we are disconnected from the God Port, the reason for our small band width capacity between us and God through the Holy Spirit.

Think about it…

If we truly believed God's word, His every word and every promise what would keep us away from Him?

Anything?

Do we know His every word and promise?

I can't list them all here because His entire book is full of them but let me enlighten you with a few in order to encourage you to go into His word on your own and begin to uncover His promises for you and increase your capacity to consume God's messages coming through the God Port.

> *"And we know that in all things God works for the good of those who love him, who have been called according to his purpose. For those God foreknew he also predestined to be conformed to the likeness of his Son, that he might be the firstborn among many brothers. And those he predestined, he also called; those he called he also justified; those he justified, he also glorified. What, then, shall we say in response to this? If God is for us, who can be against us? He who did not spare his own Son, but gave him up for us all...how will he not also, along with him, graciously give us all things? Who will bring any charge against those whom God has chosen? It is God who justifies. Who is he that condemns? Christ Jesus, who died...more than that, who was raised to life...is at the right hand of God and is also interceding for us. Who shall separate us from the love of Christ? Shall trouble or hardship or persecution or famine or nakedness or danger or sword? As it is written:*
>
> *For your sake we face death all day long; we are considered as sheep to be slaughtered.*
>
> *No, in all these things we are more than conquerors through him who loves us. For I am convinced that neither death nor life, neither angels nor demons, neither the present nor the future, nor any powers, neither height nor depth nor anything else in all creation, will be able to separate us from the love of God that is in Christ Jesus our Lord."*
>
> - Romans 8:28-38

Did you see all that, this passage is packed with promises and the wonders of God's love for us. The first sentence in the verse says God causes (NAS translation) all things to work together for good to those who love God.

Not some things, not a few things, all things. What does that mean...*all things*?

The passage says God foreknew us, predestined us and conformed us to the likeness of His Son. God knew us before we were born, he placed us here at this time for such a time as this (predestined) and He made us in Christ's image (conformed).

That sounds like a pretty good start to me but what does that mean?

> *"I pray also that the eyes of your heart may be enlightened in order that you may know the hope to which he has called you, the riches of his glorious inheritance in the saints, and his incomparably great power for us who believe.*
>
> *That power is like the working of his mighty strength, which he exerted in Christ when he raised him from the dead and seated him at his right hand in the heavenly realms, far above all rule and authority, power and dominion, and every title that can be given, not only in the present age but also in the one to come."* Ephesians 1:18-26

Do we believe that, really believe it?

We have the same power in us that God used to raise Christ from the dead and seat him in the heavenly realm. Do we really believe this, if we did wouldn't the world look different today then it does? If we were moving in the full power of God almighty as He says we have what would that mean, how could that transform our families, our communities our nations?

Would disease be able to manifest itself in this environment, would the poor go hungry?

No!

The lame would walk, the blind would see and the widows and orphans would be satisfied at the city gates.

Are you beginning to see and sense and feel the power of His word?

Jesus said it himself, *"It is written: 'Man does not live on bread alone, but on every word that comes from the mouth of God.'"*

> *"Consequently, faith comes from hearing the message, and the message is heard through the word of Christ."* Romans 10:17

We all want the easy fix, the magic formula to achieve our dreams and desires that we overlook the simple, the obvious. God's word is packed with "how to's" to achieve exactly what we are looking for we just don't realize what that is, God! We are looking for God and the power we have in Him through Christ.

We are searching for our purpose for living, our reason for being here and strength to endure the hardships that come before us.

> *"For this very reason, make every effort to add to your faith goodness; and to goodness, knowledge; and to knowledge, self —control; and to self-control, perseverance; and to perseverance, godliness; and to godliness, brotherly kindness; and to brotherly kindness, love.*
>
> *For if you posses these qualities in* **increasing measure**, *they will keep you from being ineffective and unproductive in your knowledge of our Lord Jesus Christ.*
>
> *But if anyone does not have them, he is nearsighted and blind, and has forgotten that he has been cleansed from his past sins."* 2 Peter 1:5-9

Here it is the formula for productivity and effectiveness in life - as you increase goodness, knowledge, brotherly love, etc… you become more effective in all that you do!

More effective at raising your children, going to school, building relationships, loving others and truly advancing the Kingdom of God in your circle of influence and sphere that God has placed you in.

Being productive for the Kingdom of God and fulfilling the great commandment and commission!

But how many of us are stopped because of the last part of this passage? We have forgotten that he has cleansed us from our past sins!

If we have forgotten this then it is a brick in our firewall that needs to be removed to allow access to the God Port.

The other part of this verse was to attain these qualities in increasing measure that implies we have to continue growing, learning, and expanding our capabilities. You have to be alive in Christ and increasing your knowledge of God by walking daily plugged in to the God Port, which will increase your measure of each of these things.

You cannot spend quality time with God and not increase in these things because they are the things of God.

Friends, if we do not read God's word, we cannot build our belief in His promises because we won't know what they are, we cannot access something we do not know about. Besides what is the best way to remove the bricks in your firewall?

By reading God's words, establishing them as truth, and blasting away all the lies of the enemy that are stacked up as bricks now!

How do we increase our faith, by hearing the word of God? Here is an official "tip" since I know you have been looking for one, read God's word out loud!

How can you increase your faith by hearing God's word if you don't hear it?

When you read God's word aloud you are invoking more of your senses and you are activating your faith by hearing His word.

This one "tip" will change your bible reading time and begin to bring the joy of the Lord into this time so you will naturally want to spend more time in His word. As you read the word aloud you are opening the God Port for two way communication and allowing God a greater opportunity to return revelation and wisdom and understanding back to you.

As we get God's word in our spirit and our heart and our mind we are armed and positioned to withstand everything the enemy can throw at us.

The Holy Spirit recalls the word back to us as we need it for any situation but if we don't know it then it cannot be recalled.

Remember how Jesus triumphed over temptation in the desert from Satan?

He quoted God's word back to Satan.

If we are learning to listen to God's voice and we have not studied His word, how do we know it is His voice? There are many voices at times running around in our heads (or is that just my head?) and being able to hear God's voice amongst the noise is critical.

Spending time in His word, getting to know Him through His word will distinguish those voices and let God's voice ring loud and clear. The word of God brings clarity to our thoughts so we can be obedient to God.

> *"We are destroying speculations and every lofty thing raised up against the knowledge of God and we are taking every thought captive to the obedience of Christ."* 2 Corinthians 10:5

How can we take every thought captive to the obedience of Christ if we can't distinguish God's voice and God's word from the rest of the noise?

God's voice is obedient to Christ because they are one, but Satan's voice is not obedient, our voice is not always obedient, the voices of shame, guilt and discontent are not obedient to Christ.

Knowing the word of God is the missing piece of truly hearing and knowing God's voice and being obedient to it.

Walking it Out

What I have realized in my journey is that while I was often hearing the voice of God, I did not truly know the voice of God.

Time in His word has brought me to not just hearing but knowing His voice. It's a deeper place of intimacy with God and once you experience it you will not want to go back to the shallow places again!

Knowing the voice of God has truly increased my bandwidth and my capacity to consume and God has responded by sending me more revelation and allowing the Holy Spirit to decrypt deeper meanings and messages as I have prepared myself to be able to receive them through the God Port.

I always told God that I would be happy to be obedient if I just knew which voice was His!

I hope others can relate to this thought and it's not just me.

Our heads can get really noisy with the things of the world, man's ideas, the media, the economy, our jobs, our families our responsibilities. As we spend more time in God's word and begin to really "marinate" in His word, we begin to believe what He says is true; we begin to believe His word and His vision for our lives.

And guess what His word calms the head noise so you can hear Him. His word removes doubt and reason and replaces it with peace, joy and righteousness.

If I can sum up the single most important thing I have learned in my journey it would be this:

If things are going well in your life, spend more time with God. If things are not going well in your life, spend more time with God.

Action Items

Reflect: What bible verses do you know; can you state any from memory?

What impact do they have when you quote them? Do they bring power and purpose as you state them?

When you quote scripture do you read it out loud?

Do you say it like you believe it? How much time do you spend reading God's word?

_____
_____
_____
_____
_____
_____

Pray: *Lord bring a hunger into this reader's spirit for your word, for the truths that lay with in them and for the life that it brings. Lord let your word resonate in their hearts and bring power to their vision, their purpose and their life.*

Lord bring your word to life for this reader, let each verse they read come alive before them, revealing your mysteries and power and love to them.

Lord strengthen this reader with a belief, a true belief in your word and the power that they have in You.

Continue this prayer with your own words to God, *King of Kings and Lord of Lords, you are the alpha and the omega, the beginning and the end. Your word is true and living and more powerful than a two-edge sword.*

Lord help me ....

Do: Write down a few things you would like to be more effective at.

Search your heart, listen to what God is speaking to you.

God, I would like to be more effective in:

_____
_____
_____
_____
_____
_____

Write: Write out your thoughts below. What was God showing you and speaking to you? Just start writing and allow the Holy Spirit to flow through you. One word, one sentence, one paragraph whatever comes to mind.

_____
_____
_____
_____
_____
_____
_____
_____
_____
_____
_____
_____
_____
_____
_____
_____
_____

Chapter Seven

Dial up versus High-Speed - How are we trying to connect?

Here is where the "magic" formula would come in if I had one!

The 7 Steps to Mastering the God Port!

Top 10 tips for Hearing God's Voice!

Achieving your Destiny is as easy as 1-2-3!

Now, some of you are reading this book looking for the "magic" formula, I know because I was doing the same thing!

There is no magic formula only a simple truth.

> *"Those that desire communion with God must keep their spirits quiet and serene. All hurry of spirit and turbulent passions make us unfit for divine visitations." - John Wesley*

The third and probably hardest aspect of spending time with God is really just spending time with Him. When we first start this process it is like accessing the internet via a dial-up modem.

Remember those days?

You click on your little phone icon on your desktop computer, you listen to the sounds of the modem, first dialing, then screeching at you then dinging then silence.

Ah silence you are now connected.

You go to a website and wait ever so patiently for the page to load, the pictures and information to appear.

You might open your email and go get a cup of coffee while you wait for it to finish opening.

You are patient because you don't know any other speed, you are just delighted with the overall ability you have once you get connected. You time your work and day around dial up speeds and you accept it all the while thinking it is the best thing since sliced bread.

Now, you don't want to have to dial up too many times in the day because of the time it takes so you bundle all of your tasks that require a connection together and try to do them all while you are already connected.

We were patient in this process because we didn't know any different; we didn't know higher speeds were coming so we settled for dial up. But, then we went to work one day and offered high-speed access because you could get your job done better and faster with direct access to the internet.

You could be more efficient and effective because getting on the internet improved your work flow and your processes.

You didn't have to dial up anymore you could just open your browser window and be there, online, all the time.

How great was this, you thought!

Then you went home at night and had to connect again via your dial up, so slow, so painful and you grew impatient, frustrated and annoyed. You wanted those same speeds at home that you experienced at work.

Eventually as technology allowed and budget allowed you got rid of the dial up and graduated to high speed, on all the time.

Life was good again and you would never go back to dial up!

So now we are plugged in all the time, via our computers, our cell phones and our iPods. We are streaming tv, videos and music from all devices from the internet and we can stay connected.

We are Facebooking, and tweeting, and retweeting.

We have bought into the high-speed lies of the world, fast food, fast cars and fast internet. We want everything now, now, now and we have tried to apply this to our relationship with God!

Or…was that just me?

Here is where we have to go back a step in technology, back to dial-up speeds for awhile and learn to patiently wait for the next page to load, the images to come flooding down and the information to appear before our eyes.

Is anyone else thinking about a turtle?

We need to think about time in relationship to God and His timing rather than the worlds. He created the world in seven days.

Do you think His seven days are the same as ours?

The world says differently, we have obligations and responsibilities that require us to keep moving. We can't slow down or we will get ran over, we can't get up any earlier because we need our sleep but we can stay up late chatting with friends on Facebook.

We have rationalized God right out of our lives because of time, yet God does not know time, and is not bound by it.

Even worse, I rationalized that I was seeking him, I went to church, I paid my tithes, I gave to good causes and I loved Him. Those are all good things, and those are things God has given us a heart for…but they are *not* spending time with God.

God says we are saved by grace and no good works is necessary so that can't be the key to spending time with him but how many of us have tried this very thing.

> *"For it is by grace you have been saved, through faith...and this not from yourselves, it is the gift of God...not by works, so that no one can boast."* Ephesians 2:8-9

But God also says "Seek me with all your heart."

Can we truly do this if we only spend a few minutes in the morning on our way to work?

Can we truly do this if our only time with him is Sunday at church?

Can we truly do this if we only talk to him in the shower, or at the line in the grocery store or while we are working out at the gym?

Really can we?

Now I'm not saying all these things aren't good or right they are but where is your quiet time with Him, where is your extended time with Him? Hear this and hear this now, God is calling us to go deeper with Him, and to go deeper we need to spend more time with Him.

More quiet, uninterrupted time with God!

We need to allow ourselves time with God, letting Him speak to us without the noise, letting Him be first!

If we will do this first then all those other times we mentioned will be even better! Its not that we can't hear Him while we are doing all those things but if that is the only time we are giving God to speak to us then we can't tune in as easily and quickly.

If you want port 3303 open all the time, God's voice flowing and speaking to you every moment of every day then take time with Him now, start with dial up speeds and let God bring the acceleration.

Make God first in your life, first before the dishes, the soccer game, the commute, the hair dresser and that dinner out.

Make Him first before work, before breakfast and before the "noise" of the day presses in.

Make Him first before the newspaper, the morning news and the today show.

Make Him first and then all the stuff in the middle becomes more precious jewels and gems!

Those moments are deep and fulfilling, they are revelatory, and discerning - they are direct connections all day.

Now your port stays open, now your port is processing higher band width because there is more traffic and longer streams of data coming from God every moment.

Now instead of a few brief transactions a day with God you have one continuous stream flowing and pouring out revelation to you all day long! While in the beginning it seems a sacrifice whether you are getting up early, going to bed late to spend time with Him or some other time in the day it is worth it. As we honor God with our time, He honors us with His blessings, His promises and His word.

In the end God doesn't want our hour a day and we are done, God wants us moving in His revelation all day long, God wants us accessing Him, listening to Him and moving in His power and might at all times.

You see as you persevere with your time with God He develops that into a natural 24/7 access and open communication, The God Port bursts wide open and now you have high-speed access!

As this happens then our "quiet" time with Him becomes a joy to us because now we are yearning for it and we are walking in the fruit of it and we want more of Him.

We must put God first in our lives if we are to complete the good work He has placed before us.

How can we hear His voice if we don't spend time getting to know what it sounds like? We spend years with our family and friends which allows us to recognize their voice on the phone, their steps up the walk and their faces in a crowd.

How much time do we spend with our creator, the Lord God almighty?

Do we dwell in His word?

Do we seek Him in prayers?

Do we seek His face?

If not, then how can we recognize His voice?

How can we expect to distinguish His voice from the others we hear if we haven't spent time getting to know Him?

Psalm 46:10 says, *"Be still, and know that I am God"*.

What does this mean, and how do we accomplish this?

This is the dial-up speed I was referring to; our quiet time with God should be unrushed and completely surrendered to Him. I believe we do not allow ourselves this privilege.

We are geared by the world to stay moving, keep busy, act now, act fast, don't miss out, these are the messages coming at us. God's word says "Be still."

The word 'still' is defined as remaining in place or at rest; motionless; stationary; free from sound or noise, silent; subdued, free from turbulence or commotion; peaceful; tranquil; or calm just to name a few.

The word *be* is defined as to occupy a place or position; to belong, attend or befall. So if we put these together we might get be still means to "attend at rest; belong free from sound or noise; occupy a place of peace; befall motionless."

I love this last one.

When was the last time you were completely motionless before God, not striving to achieve, to do or to be but just completely motionless before Him? Listening and waiting on Him?

Quiet, not asking or demanding anything but seeking Him and what He wants to share with you, what He wants to say?

This kind of time was new to me; I had no idea how to do it or where to start and I was impatient, I wanted it all to work now! I got up real early and sat motionless before God, completely calm and at peace, waiting for divine visitation and revelation my first day!

Do you know what happened?

Did thunder and lightening strike?

No.

Did God descend on a cloud and sit before me?

No.

Did I hear a loud audible voice saying "This is the Lord your God"?

No!

As calm and tranquility overtook me, as the noise stopped and I began to be still, as I cleared my head of the worldly thoughts, yes you guessed it, I fell asleep!

This is where my journey started, I had a long way to go but I was determined. I say this to encourage you, start where you are and lean unto God for understanding and direction.

Be patient and accept dial up speeds for a season. He taught me and continues to teach me about "being still" before Him, He will teach you as you press in and persevere, He will commune with you, He will come alongside you and He will speak to you.

The God Port will be opened, and streams of living water will pour out and increase download speeds.

When I first began really trying to press into God I did what I heard others did. Get up early, read the bible and pray.

All excellent things, but I wasn't applying my "uniqueness's – how God wired me" to the situation. I was trying to do it like everyone else and guess what?

It was frustrating and unfruitful.

However, instead of giving up I just kept trying. And I say trying for a reason because it was by trial and error that I learned what worked for me with God.

God is always the same; always unchanging and so is His word. However, how we commune with Him, how we connect with Him and plug into our Port 3303 will be different because we are different. We are unique, and we are exactly what God designed in us - a unique combination of natural talent, skills and gifting combined in a unique DNA to be able to do what God has predestined us for.

After my first week of frustrations and failures of spending time with God I began pulling books off my shelves and reading them, books on how to hear God's voice and knowing God's will.

One of these books reminded me of something my girlfriend had been encouraging me to do for years…keep a journal!

She said that journaling helps allow the flow of the Holy Spirit to come and for God's voice to speak to us without our logical, analytical mind getting in the way.

I had been bucking this idea for years. I spent plenty of time in college writing notes and essays and term papers and was done writing, or so I thought! I decided there was no harm in trying this journaling thing, so I bought a few notebooks and got started. I figured the least it could do was help keep me awake in the early hours.

Guess what…journaling works!

It gave me something to do during my quiet time with God, which was huge for me. In the beginning, the journaling was similar to my prayers just writing what I was thinking and praying about, it seemed silly to me but I persisted. I wanted to spend time with God and I knew I had to stay awake to do this.

Although there were a few mornings where I prayed for divine visitation and dreams, as I dozed off to sleep!

My journaling evolved just like my prayers and my bible studies. As I began writing my words to God, they would become His words to me. I can't explain how this happens just that it does. As we just let the words flow to paper our brain get's out of the way and pretty soon the words flowing are from God.

The first few times I experienced this I had trouble believing that I hadn't somehow orchestrated it all but I just kept writing.

After my first journal filled up I went back through it and read it again. I found revelation, inspiration and directions from God hidden like buried treasure.

I gleaned these insights out of my journal and wrote them down in a separate notebook. I knew they were visions and directions from God and needed to be on a list. Every few months now as I finish a journal I read back through it, pull the gems and nuggets out from the Lord and put them on a list.

I review this list as God directs and act on the items as I feel the Lord leading.

There are usually several things that have already been accomplished by the time I get to this step and several that I see bubbling up in my life at that time and a few that I know are future actions and assignments that just need to sit and simmer.

I can't believe I waited so many years to start spending quiet time with the Lord and using journaling to help me.

As we learn to press into the Lord and spend time with Him He reveals great and mighty things to us. God is looking for those that are pressed in and trusting Him and listening to Him to call them into their purpose to advance His Kingdom.

God wants His Kingdom, His government prepared and established here on earth so that heaven can invade!

We have discussed that there is no magic formula and no fool proof seven-step plan to hearing God's voice. There is one simple approach, one simple command, and one desire from God that if we fulfill it, He will fulfill all He has promised.

He wants our time, our hearts our thoughts.

God created man and placed him here on earth to have dominion and to establish heaven on earth isn't it time we get started on our assignment?

> *"For I know the plans I have for you," declares the Lord, "plans to prosper you and not to harm you, plans to give you hope and a future. Then you will call upon me and come and pray to me, and I will listen to you. You will seek me and find me when you seek me with all your heart."* Jeremiah 29:11-14

God created man in His own image because He wanted relationship with us and intimacy from His creation.

God moves in the spiritual realm, the spiritual dimension, there is no time to God, God is time and God wants our time. We are here but for a moment compared to eternity and God wants our time and attention while we are so that we might accomplish all He has predestined us for.

> *"We, do, however, speak a message of wisdom among the mature, but not the wisdom of this age or of the rulers of this age; who are coming to nothing. No, we speak of God's secret wisdom, a wisdom that has been hidden and that God destined for our glory before time began."*
> - I Corinthians 2:6-7

We have to really understand the idea of eternity and heaven here on earth in order to be able to prioritize our day according to God's will for us.

We are called to sacrifice ourselves for our Father in Heaven but do we?

Have we?

Have we done all to stand and remained standing?

> *"Therefore put on the full armor of God, so that when the day of evil comes, you may be able to stand your ground, and after you have done everything, to stand."* Ephesians 6:13

I said there is no magic formula, but there is an easy answer, a simple solution...one so simple, in fact, it doesn't seem it can be real, but it is.

We must plug into The God Port without any interference so we can pursue Him with our whole heart, with the type of pursuit that we have probably experimented with and dabbled at over the years but have not persevered through.

We must get directly connected to the Lord our God, we must turn down the noise of the world so we can hear Him.

We must leave the distractions behind and go "within".

We must go deeper into ourselves where the Holy Spirit is waiting and listening and speaking and decrypting the messages of God.

We must give God our time in dial up speeds and He will give back so much more in high-speed and accelerate us into His future!

Here is the good news and the bad news it is up to you! I can provide you with insights, steps and ideas on how to begin pressing in, I can share my story of what worked and didn't work for me to encourage you along the way, but rest assured until you start your own journey, until you begin spending more time with God, it won't happen for you.

Nothing replaces our dedicated, in the garden time with the Lord. Conferences, books, cd's, etc… bring encouragement, give direction, provide tools and help bring understanding and is part of the pursuit.

It's that one on one time with the Lord that will bring transformation, a deepening of our belief and an opening of our God Port.

Walking it Out

I was talking with one of my mentors the other day about still struggling with the "be still" portion of my time with the Lord.

I happily worship, pray, sing songs and jump around my office but the "be still" continues to be difficult for me.

As we began talking I realized that my "be still" time is coming throughout the day at moments I least expect it or am trying to achieve it. I have always worked tirelessly for my employer and now in my business so being still during the work day is not a common occurrence for me.

However as I have spent more time with the Lord in the morning, getting grounded and set for the day I find more quiet times throughout the day where I am truly still before the Lord.

We try so hard to do things like we think God wants us to do them or like other people do them but it's absolutely true that we are all unique. Allow the uniqueness of God in you to come through you as you pursue Him.

I met with Lee Domingue, author of "Pearls of the King," to ask him how he spent time with the Lord. I had heard him speak at a conference and I sensed God's peace and joy on his life. After reading his book I felt led by the Lord to meet him and spend some time with him. Lee runs a $100 million company yet he was gracious and accepting of my invitation to meet with him. I scheduled a whirlwind trip to Louisiana and flew the red eye to get there.

This was one of those divine appointments from God that seemed crazy, but I had to go.

When Lee and I sat down, and I asked him what his time with the Lord looked like and what he did, he immediately got up and grabbed his bible. Our time together instantly shifted from interview and chat to a deep intimate time together with the Lord. He read scripture, we talked, he shared, God joined us and two hours later we were both running late.

I not only got to meet him but I had the privilege of experiencing his time with the Lord with him! What I realized is that Lee's God Port was wide open and all his time was with God, there was no separation.

Lee understood what it meant to be still before the Lord and it showed in everything else he put his hand to. He didn't struggle with opening the God Port; it was always on, always open and always sending and receiving. He was where I was striving to get and God was showing me it was possible.

God was showing me the desire of my heart and giving me a glimpse of what was to come as I persevered in Him.

Action Items

Reflect: Do you know how to "be still" before God? When was the last time you spent time with God with no expectations? Do you ask God to order your day and layout His priorities for you?

Do you rush through your time with God like you do a fast food drive-up?

Pray: *Lord thank you for your patience with us. You spend an eternity waiting upon us to choose you, to seek you, to spend time with you and you never leave us or forsake us.*

Lord show this reader how you want to spend quiet time with them.

Teach them how to quiet themselves before you and enjoy spending time with you without expectation of return but rather just enjoying the company of a friend, a father, a loved one. .

Continue this prayer with your own words to God, *My Lord, My Father in heaven praise you and thank you for your unconditional and never ending love for me. Lord still my heart and thoughts before you that I might …*

Do: Decide right now where you will spend your quiet time with the Lord. Choose a specific location in your house or your office or wherever is most suitable for uninterrupted time with God.

My Location: _____

Write: Write out your thoughts below. What was God showing you and speaking to you? Just start writing and allow the Holy Spirit to flow through you. One word, one sentence, one paragraph whatever comes to mind.

_____
_____
_____
_____
_____
_____
_____
_____
_____
_____
_____
_____
_____
_____
_____
_____
_____

Chapter Eight
Page Cannot be Found – What are we missing?

Sometimes when I search the web I click on a link to a page and I get an error message that says, page cannot be found.

I get frustrated and annoyed that the link is old and no longer points to an active page. I think why didn't someone make sure that link got updated with the last website changes or why doesn't the company check their website and make sure all the pages are working?

I think to myself well if they can't keep their website working how well will they do helping me with my problem?

Do you think God ever thinks this way about us?

He certainly has the right to don't you think!

Do you ever feel this way about God?

Why isn't He there listening to me and answering my prayers?

It feels sometimes like He cannot be found. Who do you think is really missing something, us…or God?

Do you ever find yourself acting in ways that you know are not Christ like and regretting your behavior or actions?

Do you find yourself apologizing to God for the same sins over and over again?

Are your prayers just a constant one way communication to God of all the things He needs to fix for you?

What do you think the missing page is in our walk with Christ, in our search for Him, in our quest?

I believe what is missing is true transformation!

> *"And be not conformed to this world: but be ye transformed by the renewing of your mind, that ye may prove what is that good, and acceptable, and perfect, will of God."* Romans 12:2

Let's look at this verse in another translation, the New Living translation says:

"Don't copy the behavior and customs of this world, but let God transform you into a new person by changing the way you think. Then you will learn to know God's will for you, which is good and pleasing and perfect."

I love this verse in all of its translations, it is the missing key, the thing that will either launch you into your calling and election or keep you from it!

We must renew our minds; we must not be conformed to this world but rather transformed.

How does this happen?

Have you heard the saying that the books you read, the people you surround yourself with and the things you listen to will be where you are in five years?

Do you think there is something to this?

What this is referring to is that where you spend your time and what you think about conforms you to those things.

If you want to be more like Jesus and truly be transformed what should you be readying and who should you be hanging out with?

I struggled for years with the same patterns of behavior all the while praying God would fix me and change them but guess what nothing changed!

However when I started spending time with God, reading His word and seeking Him, my mind was renewed and I began to experience true transformation.

I say true transformation because I went from striving to change to being changed!

Trust me as long as we strive in our own strength and efforts we will always fail, we will always fall short and we will walk in frustration instead of the joy of the Lord. When we focus on the things of God by spending time with God, our minds are renewed, our thinking is changed and we can't help but be transformed.

Now, instead of striving in your own strength you are walking in the likeness of Christ and the power of the Most High God.

Trust me there is much more peace in this place of true transformation and you will begin to experience the joy, peace and righteousness God's word talks about.

> *"For the Kingdom of God is not a matter of eating and drinking, but of righteousness, peace and joy in the Holy Spirit.* Romans 14:17

Why are more Christians not walking in their calling, why is the idea of Christianity looked down upon and discounted?

I believe it is because we are not truly transformed and walking in that transformation. The world is not seeing the fruit of our transformation which is joy, peace and righteousness, so what is in it for them?

We are called to be salt and light but if we are missing the transformation then frankly Christianity is just a lot of work without any fruit!

Are you tired of this struggle like I was?

Do you want to live in the fullness of Christ and be the salt and light you are called to be?

Then press into God, give Him your time and experience true transformation and the peace, joy and righteousness will be a natural outpouring.

Are we living transformed, do our deeds and actions display to the world that we are transformed?

How can we be transformed by the renewing of our minds if we are not pressed into that which renews us?

The renewing of our minds comes from communing with God through praise, worship, prayer, reading His word and quiet time. The transformation happens when we learn to open the God port and stay plugged into the things of God.

As we hear the word of God spoken to us, breathed into us from the spirit then the renewing can take place and as his word says as we are renewed in our minds, we are transformed. Getting saved gets you eternal life and is the beginning of our walk with Christ.

The renewing of our minds, the transformation comes as we journey together with God. So many people stop short of the goal line and miss the best part; the transformation, the power and might of God in their lives. This is the missing piece in believer's lives today and it is this piece that is needed to bring others to Christ.

If we say we are living for Christ but don't wear His Glory then why would others want to receive what we have?

We have been so busy teaching and preaching the Gospel of Salvation that we have missed the next step, preaching and teaching the Gospel of the Kingdom!

Walking it Out

I spent years trying to be good, trying to make good decisions, trying not to sin, trying to be a better person, trying to be a good mom and wife, trying to be a good Christian!

The more I tried in my own strength the more I seemed to fail and the more I felt like I disappointed God.

As I began spending more time with God, pressing in and seeking His voice there was an unexpected outcome, less struggles with annoying bad habits! I had always struggled with losing weight, exercising regularly and a myriad of other goals I could never quite reach. I remember as I started pressing in I tried to add these to the list of goals and God was very clear, no other goal except spending more time with Him.

As I focused on that one objective, the other outcomes eventually came naturally; finally true transformation had begun because it was not in my own strength but the fruit of my time with God.

I began to truly reap the "all other things shall be added", I was delighted and amazed and wondering why I had waited so long in truly seeking the Lord. I started spending concentrated time with God in September, in January I began exercising and by June I had lost 25 pounds with very little effort. A year later I have still maintained that weight loss and exercise.

My mind was being renewed every day by the word of God, by His presence and His voice and for the first time I really began to understand what transformation was all about.

The fruit of the spirit is peace, joy and righteousness and for the first time I was spending more time walking in this fruit then in my own short comings, guilt and shame. It was and is a great place to be and I spend more time with God each day in hopes to stay in this place and walk out what God has for me.

Is transformation ever complete?

I don't believe so, but as we stay faithful to the Lord and His calling on our lives we can stay in this place of continual transformation and He will increase our responsibility in advancing His kingdom.

I realized I had finally moved past "working out my salvation" to walking in the kingdom, what a glorious transformation this is! Jesus never preached on salvation He preached on the kingdom. His first sermon spoke about the kingdom of heaven is at hand or near.

Transformation from striving to do good in our own strength to living as a king in God's kingdom is a monumental shift.

We are truly citizen's of heaven and as we truly believe that and begin to walk in that, we walk in the victory God gave us through His son and become salt and light in whatever circle of influence God has called us to.

Action Items

Reflect: Do you ever think you are not good enough to hear God's voice or spend time with Him? Do you feel like you are constantly disappointing God? Do you find yourself praying on Sunday to do better this next week, to spend more time with God and more time reading your bible?

Pray: *Lord thank you for this reader, thank you for your love that you are lavishing upon them. Lord speak to their hearts, show them how much you love them and free them up from their shame and guilt.*

Lord shame and guilt are not from you but rather joy, peace and righteousness. Pour out your joy and peace on this reader so they might walk in that joy and peace as you renew their thinking. Lord raise up their thinking to know they are part of your kingdom, they are a citizen in your kingdom and they are a king called to an assignment that only they can fulfill.

Continue this prayer with your own words to God, *Lord change my thinking from what I have done wrong to who I am in you. Help me to walk in your victory every day and to be transformed by the renewing of my mind. Lord I lay everything at your feet…*

Do: Choose your strength verse from the bible. A verse that encourages you when you are down, a verse that reminds you of who you are in Christ, a verse that you can memorize and draw upon throughout your day and week to stay grounded in your thinking on the things of God.

Write it down and memorize it. Feel free to draw on all the verses I have used in The God Port, they are all listed in the back of the book under bible references.

My Strength Verse

_____
_____
_____

Write: Write out your thoughts below.

What was God showing you and speaking to you?

Just start writing and allow the Holy Spirit to flow through you. One word, one sentence, one paragraph whatever comes to mind.

_____
_____
_____
_____
_____

Chapter Nine
URL – What's yours?

URL stands for unique resource locator, in technology the url is the name by which you find a website and every website has a unique name and a unique address i.e. a unique URL.

God made us unique, our heart beat, our finger prints, and every hair on our head. If we are unique in all these ways don't you think our time with God will be unique too?

Don't you think our URL to and from God is unique?

Discovering the God port is about discovering your URL to God, your unique resource locator, your unique method and process for connecting to the God port. If we are all to make up the body of Christ, we all have to have our own unique skill set to add to what the body needs.

If we all had the DNA to make up a toe, the body would be sorely lacking in the other things it needs to function. In as much as we are unique and different so is our time with God.

What makes us tick, what helps us listen and learn, what helps us press into God is different. What does it mean for us to "Be still and know that I am God"?

I don't know what it is for you but you and God do, it's a journey of discovery. This book is to help you get started on the journey, to get started pressing in to the Lord and to begin to understand and believe what God's word says is true.

This book is meant to be a guideline, a help to get started and begin hearing God's voice and opening your God Port.

As followers of Christ we all have the same purpose, the same mandate, go into all the world and teach the good news. That is every believer's purpose, the great commission that God calls us all to as we accept Jesus as our Lord and Savior.

> *"He sad to them, go into all the world and preach the good news to all creation."* Mark 16:15

However how we achieve that purpose is different for each of us, this is our "calling" our "election" our URL!

Remember God made us all unique with just the right combinations of skills, abilities, giftings and talents to do what we were predestined for.

> *"Therefore, my brothers, be all the more eager to make your calling and election sure. For if you do these things, you will never fall and you will receive a rich welcome into the eternal kingdom of our Lord and Savior Jesus Christ."* II Peter 1:10

Imagine what the world would look like, what our communities would be like if all Christians were moving in the full power and might of God through their calling and election.

In other words if we were all connected to our URL with God and operating in our full gifts to accomplish what we were predestined to do, how would that impact our families, our communities, our workplace, our nation and all the nations?

What if those called to leadership in the cultural influencers of our nation were Christians moving in their calling?

City councilmen and school board members, government leaders, teachers, business people, media professionals, artists and entertainers, church leaders, parents and family members.

Do you think prayer would have been taken out of the schools or the Ten Commandments taken out of our courtrooms?

Would judges be legislating from the bench instead of upholding the constitution?

We must walk in the righteousness of Christ in all areas of our life according to our uniqueness and our influence to bring the hope of His glory to all men.

As we demonstrate and uphold the righteousness of Christ the world will be changed and God will be glorified.

Walking it Out

I have always known I was called to be in business, to work and to spend the majority of my time in the marketplace yet I never felt released or equipped from my church body.

I felt pulled out of the marketplace and into the church to be in "full-time" ministry to use my gifts. Yet I felt like I was using them already in the marketplace, leading bible studies, praying with co-workers and encouraging those around me.

As I pressed into the Lord and opened the God port He began to confirm my calling and election, He showed me my unique URL and led me to divine appointments and connections to help me expand those gifts and equip me for the unique calling He had on my life.

What I began to realize is that He had been equipping me my whole life.

All that I had been through; all that I had learned the easy way and the hard way, all the work experience and life experience was for this moment, for a time such as this.

God is moving mightily in the marketplace, He is calling His marketplace believers together to raise them up to be the kings He has called us to be.

Yes, we are kings in His kingdom and as we gather together and each step into our calling and election God will use us to advance His kingdom through our marketplace influence.

As we press into Him, He will reveal himself through us so that He might be glorified in all that we do. As we honor Christ in the marketplace He will expand our influence and increase our responsibility so that His kingdom can be advanced.

Imagine if all those in the marketplace were moving in their full gifting and talents, walking out their kingdom assignments and marching forward together as the kings they have been called to be.

How different would things be, what kind of impact could they have?

Could this nation be changed, could other nations be changed, could God's righteousness flow through the land once again, yes, absolutely yes!

You see it is our responsibility to take up our assignment and use our unique combination of skills, talent, gifts and abilities to advance His kingdom, to press into God and prepare ourselves for all that He is calling us to.

If not now, when, if not you, who?

Opening the God port is a wild, exciting ride and I would never want to go back to the confusion of all the other voices again! I can now hear God and I know it is Him, what a refreshing and reassuring place to be.

I encourage you to join me. Is it always easy, no, is it always predictable and what you expect, absolutely not.

Is it worth it?

Absolutely!

Whether you are called to pasturing a church, raising a family, being a journalist, actor, congressman, school teacher or business owner, if you are moving in your calling and election, you will not fall.

It is in God's word.

We are all called to carry out the great commission and share the good news but how we each do it is unique to us.

God has given us a wonderful combination of skills, talents, gifts and abilities to achieve the assignment He is calling us to.

Embrace your gifting, skills and talents, don't hide them under a rock and seek your assignment from God. Press in to God, open your God Port and let Him guide you in making your calling and election sure!

As you press in to Him your gifts become honed and they begin to bear fruit to advance the Kingdom.

Action Items

Reflect: What are your unique set of skills, giftings and abilities? What comes easily for you?

What do you enjoy doing? What makes your heart sing?

What stirs your heart when you think about it?

Pray: *Lord thank you for this reader's unique make-up that only you could achieve. For the rate at which their heart beats, for the number of hairs on their head and for the unique blend of all you are in them.*

Lord thank you for their skills, their talents and help them uncover these talents and giftings to be used for your kingdom.

Lord bless this reader and all they put their hands to that you would be honored and glorified through everything they do.

Continue this prayer with your own words to God, *Lord show me how you have made me unique and the skills you have given me to accomplish all that you have called me to.*

Lord thank you for my ability to …

Do: Write down one or two things that come easy to you.

My Skills:

_____
_____
_____
_____

Write: Write out your thoughts below. What was God showing you and speaking to you?

Just start writing and allow the Holy Spirit to flow through you. One word, one sentence, one paragraph whatever comes to mind.

_____
_____
_____
_____
_____
_____
_____
_____
_____
_____
_____
_____
_____
_____
_____
_____
_____
_____
_____
_____
_____

Chapter Ten
Go back or continue - What will you do next?

When you are on a web page you often have the choice to "go back" to a previous page or previous place you were at or you can "continue", move forward on your actions.

What you choose to do next after reading this book is this kind of choice. You can choose to "go back" to the way things were or you can choose to "continue" your journey and learn to open the God Port.

The next step is easy but monumental!

Pressing into God, spending time with Him and learning to hear His voice is an act of obedience. With that act comes commitment, perseverance and steadfastness.

God's word says: *Seek me with your whole heart and all other things shall be added unto you!*

So what is next is more time with God and acting on the words, visions, dreams and revelation He gives us. It's so simple, we spend so much time wondering and worrying about what's next, what do we do, where do we go, how do we proceed; with our families, with our lives, with our work and with our ministry.

There is only one next step for you to take, one task that lies before you, one goal to set; increase your time with God!

Now, if you are like me you are thinking about a hundred different things you want to achieve, do, goals to set, things to change and you are ready to transform your entire life by doing all of these different things at once. I know, I was at this critical next step and began thinking about all the other things to achieve as well.

God's word says, seek me and all other things shall be added.

Do you really get that and understand it?

God had to really clarify this for me and stop me in my tracks before I spiraled into the pit of unreasonable goal setting and fixing everything all at once! He said one thing to me: "Spend time with me, don't change anything else."

Wow, really only one thing?

I liked the idea of it but had trouble believing that one thing, one action, one change could get me where I wanted to go but His words were clear and strong so I chose to continue, to move forward, to take the next step.

I set aside my first hour of the day to spend with Him, nothing else. I had reams of goals rushing through my head, start exercising, lose weight, read one book a day, leave work on time, write my blog daily, build a new website, write a book and on and on and on.

My head was spinning but I heeded God's voice and just did that one thing, set aside my first hour of the day for Him.

I had no idea what to expect but of course had high expectations which as you read in an earlier chapter ended in sleep! I persevered, I refused to give up and I asked the Lord to teach me how to spend time with Him and He did.

I didn't set any other goals or decide on any other changes, just time with God. As I began having success at the one hour, I thought great I will increase it to two!

God smiled and stopped me and said not yet!

I continued for the one hour a day until it went by so fast and seemed so short and I felt frustrated that I didn't have more time to spend with Him. Now it was time to extend my morning time to two hours. The journey continued from here and I remained steadfast in the single next step, the one change, spend time with God.

After several months I noticed other things happening that I wasn't really working at or consciously trying to change.

As you still yourself, listen to the Lord, seek His visions and journal your prayers to Him and His words to you, God will bring revelation and all other things shall be added.

That's the wonder of God, the beauty of our relationship.

I continued my pursuit, my time with Him and only focusing on that one step and God began moving in my life in many areas that I had struggled with in the past. You know before the transformation when I was trying to do everything in my own strength!

Trust me; God's way is definitely easier once you get the hang of it and get yourself out of the way.

God began teaching me about stewardship and I of course thought that just meant how I handled my money (whose money?).

He showed me stewardship was so much more than just finances although I did get those specific lessons as well!

As He began to unravel the concepts of stewardship with me, He began to show me how to apply these in other areas and before I knew it, I was losing weight, eating better and turning off lights with little effort or struggle!

Walking it Out

This step is the grandest of them all.

This is where the rubber meets the road!

I knew as I sat in my car in the 100 degree heat at that conference in Austin TX, crying out to God, that this was the cross roads, the turning point. I knew this decision was huge and would have the greatest impact on my life yet!

But could I do it, could I stick with it, could I persevere and persist unlike prior trials and errors?

As I sat in my car contemplating this idea and having to admit I had not truly sought God with all my heart before, I had not put His word to practice and sought the kingdom and His righteousness first in all the years I had been a Christian.

Why hadn't I, why should I now, what would be different?

I was scared it would work and scared it wouldn't! What if it didn't and God wasn't real, what if it did and He called me to things I didn't want to do?

What did this mean for my family, my business, and my career? What if He truly wanted me to give up my business and do something else, what if He didn't?

The questions were racing through my head; the enemy was battering me like a ripped sail on the ocean. My emotions raced from prideful to defensive, to angry, to depressed, to feeling guilt and shame, to fear and to remorse. I ran the whole gambit in record time!

My head was spinning, my emotions were whirling and I was truly broken to a depth I had never been before.

I knew I could either put up those wonderful firewalls of protection or press in to God and pray it through.

I remembered why I was at the conference and began thinking about what God had been teaching me the past year about pursuing Him. It had all started when I read a blog post by Michael Pink the prior year talking about pursuing God, the title was "How Pursuing God Trumps the Pursuit of Riches – Every time!"

That sent me on the journey to understand what pursuing God meant which is revealed in my searching for God in chapter six, as God brought this back to mind I realized I was on that pursuit and this was the next step and He would not let me down.

He had led me to this place, to this cross roads, to this most important commitment; I must press in and seek Him with my whole heart, which meant time with Him.

I was on the next leg of my journey and I went from devastated to thrilled! I spent some time in prayer making my plan to spend time with God concrete and attainable, set my mind on this single goal and marched onward.

This book is the result of that decision to continue and not go back!

Action Items

Reflect: When was the last time you set a goal and achieved it? When was the last time you set a goal and didn't?

What was different about the one you achieved versus the one you didn't?

Why did you buy this book? What were you hoping to learn or achieve or conquer by reading it?

Pray: *Lord thank you for this reader that you have known before they were born. Thank you for their gifts, skills and abilities that you have given them to carry out their assignment. Lord thank you for the love you lavish upon them and have for them.*

Lord make that love more apparent and real to them right now!

Lord show them the vision you have for them and their assignment.

Lord speak to their heart right now through The God Port and encourage them to take this next step, to go deeper with you and press in to the things of God more than they have ever done before.

Lord bring a word of encouragement to them right now to take this next step and to commit spending time with you.

Continue this prayer with your own words to God, *Lord as I commit daily time with you, I thank you for meeting me, for caring for me and wanting to spend time with me. Lord thank you that you are supernatural and can be with me at all times just as you are with all your children.*

Lord as I commit …

Do: Decide right now what time every day you will spend with God. What is your daily appointment time going to be?

You chose the location in Chapter 7 now prayerfully choose your time. A time that you can control almost always so you can stay committed to that time. Decide how much time each day you will spend and I encourage you to start small and wait until the Lord releases you for more time. You will know when you are ready.

Don't over do it just decide to get started.

Note: When I first started I only focused on weekdays because my schedule was consistent and I could stay focused.

Weekends get harder and you want to start slow so you can be successful.

My Appointment Time with God: _____

My Appointment Location with God (as decided in Chapter 7 – yes you can change it now if you need to!):

_____
_____
_____

Write: Write out your thoughts below. What was God showing you and speaking to you?

Just start writing and allow the Holy Spirit to flow through you. One word, one sentence, one paragraph whatever comes to mind.

Chapter Eleven

SLA's and Uptime –
Is the return on investment (ROI) worth it?

In the world of technology and websites there has to be someone taking responsibility for keeping things up and running, internet service providers and hosting companies.

They outline their responsibilities in service level agreements (SLA) for everyone to sign and agree to.

An important component of these agreements is the "uptime" promises they make. Uptime is reported in percentages and indicates the amount of time in a month or year the responsible party is promising to keep their site up and working and available (uptime).

The greater percentage of uptime the site requires the higher the costs to achieve it.

What are our SLA's with God? What are His with us? Is it worth the price? What is the price for 100% uptime with God, 24/7 access and availability?

God already paid the price but have we?

He sent His son into the world as a sacrifice for all of us. Jesus endured beatings, torture, crucifixion and finally death on the cross for our sins. His blood was shed so that we could be saved. He was raised from the dead and seated at the right hand of God after defeating death. God sent His Holy Spirit from heaven to earth so that we would never be without Him.

This provided us the 100% uptime option in His SLA to us, 24/7 access to the God port and what was our part of the deal, our SLA to God to receive this?

By believing that Jesus was God's son and God raised him from the dead.

> *"That if you confess with your mouth, "Jesus is Lord," and believe in your heart that God raised him from the dead, you will be saved."* Romans 10:9
>
> *"If we confess our sins He (Jesus Christ) is faithful and just to forgive us our sins and to cleanse us from all unrighteousness."* 1 John 1:9
>
> *"But as many as received him, to them gave he power to become the sons of God, even to them that believe on his name."* John 1:12
>
> *"Behold I stand at your door and knock if any man hear my voice and open the door, I will come in to him and will sup with him and he with me.* Revelation 3:20

There is the mutual SLA between us and God, our part and His part. In the last verse He says He will open the door and come in.

That door is the God port.

Notice there is no time frame on how long it will be open or how long He will stay. The door is open and He comes in, 100% uptime, 24/7 access to God.

Sometimes I feel like I have spent my whole life disappointing God, making wrong choices, being self-centered and seeking the pleasures of the world over God.

Regardless of what I have done, He has always been faithful. When I was in the darkest hour of my life, God showed up and brought His light, His compassion and His strength. When I left my corporate job as sole provider of my family, God was there, meeting our financial needs every day.

When I started my business God brought clients and finances just when they were needed. When I asked the Lord a year ago to teach me how to hear His voice and to show me His heart He was there.

God paid for this SLA with His son's life, what does it cost us? Our life laid down before Him, our time, our fleshly desires, dying to self.

> *"I have been crucified with Christ and I no longer live, but Christ lives in me. The life I live in the body, I live by faith in the Son of God, who loved me and gave himself for me."* Galatians 2:20

Is it worth the price? Is giving up our time to God worth 24/7 access to Him, to hear His voice and receive revelation, wisdom and understanding in all things? Absolutely! Are there sacrifices, yes, are they worth it yes!

> *"I consider that our present sufferings are not worth comparing with the glory that will be revealed in us."* Romans 8:18

The glory that will be revealed in us, God's glory revealed in us! It's worth it.

There is no sacrifice I can make greater than the sacrifice He made for me. God sent His only son to earth, to become man to teach of His kingdom, to die on the cross, for me and for you! So really shouldn't the question be are we worth it to Him? Are we worth the heartache we cause Him?

Are we worth the disappointment He experiences when we make mistakes?

When we disregard Him?

When we ignore Him?

When we go our own way selfishly and then come crying back when things go wrong?

> *"In him we have redemption through his blood, the forgiveness of sins, in accordance with the riches of God's grace that he lavished on us with all wisdom and understanding."* Ephesians 1:7-8

Notice the words wisdom and understanding. God's grace is "lavished" on us with all of God's wisdom and understanding.

God knows who we are, God knows our short comings and weaknesses, and God knows our strengths and our idols. God knows everything about us. So, He measured out His grace for us in accordance with all that He knows.

God already paid the price for our sins through His son, so yes it is worth it to Him; we are worth it to Him, you are worth it to Him.

> *"How great is the love the Father has lavished on us, that we should be called children of God! And that is what we are!"* 1 John 3:1

There is no greater love than God's love for us.

For those of you reading this with children you understand this love to the extent humanly possible.

As a mother I can say I would die for my children. I would give up my life for them to live, to protect them, to insure their future, to keep them from harm.

Have our children ever disappointed us, sure. Will they again…probably. Do we stop loving them…no. We are to love our children unconditionally just as the Father loves us unconditionally.

Does this mean we don't discipline them?

Does this mean we don't teach them and hold them accountable for the consequences of their actions?

Does this mean we have to sometimes exercise tough love?

This is what God has done for us, already, before we were even born!

So when we come to Him regardless of where we have been, what we have been doing or what our current life looks like, He leaps for joy, His heart sings, the angels sing and He welcomes us home into His loving arms.

Walking it Out

So what does living up to our SLA to Him look like?

How do we open the God Port and receive His revelation and wisdom in all we say and do? What is the sacrifice on our part? My sacrifice was my morning time, getting up early every day whether I felt like it or not and spending time with Him.

Struggling through what that time looked like, what I should be doing and how this pressing into God really worked.

My sacrifice was early morning when I felt like He was no where around but I was there anyway, reading His word, worshipping and seeking Him.

We as humans are so often driven by our emotions that we lose sight of truth! We let our emotions run us day by day and we react to every blowing wind that passes by us. What I realized I was learning in my time with the Lord was emotional intelligence!

Learning to react to what I know to be true and not what I was feeling or others told me I should be feeling. Spending time with God and letting His word marinate in our hearts and minds provides clarity of truth that can trump emotions!

The more time I have spent reading His word the more truth I have to stand against the winds that would blow me to and fro.

The sacrifice for me has been not letting my emotions dictate what I know to be true. Daily I can react to how things "seem" or I can react to what I "know" but might be unseen.

Am I talking about faith, absolutely! Faith to believe what God has shown you is true, faith to believe His promises, faith to carry out His great commission according to our calling and election and faith to do what He is calling us to regardless of how we feel, how things look to the natural eye or what people say. My service level agreement (SLA) with God is to believe His word is true no matter what.

To walk in what I know not in what I see with the natural eye. To let the Holy Spirit guide me and not my emotions of the day.

There were many mornings when I felt like God was not there but His word says He is, His word says He will "never leave us nor forsake us" so instead of giving up and going home, I pressed in harder.

I read more scripture, I spent more time worshipping to rightly position myself in Him so I could hear Him, so I knew without a doubt He was there with me and continued to learn and seek Him and open the God Port.

I could have given up which is what my emotions were telling me but instead I persevered more in understanding Him, His truths and learning how to set emotions aside and operate in truth.

Am I there yet? No...remember it is a journey! Do I have good days and bad, yes! Do I let my emotions get the better of me sometimes, yes but do I give up...no.

I have my occasional pity party but then I remember how unpleasant they are and I realize the worst day with the Lord is better than any day without Him.

I hear Him wooing me from the God Port, rising up the Holy Spirit within me and speaking His love, His joy and His peace and righteousness to me. I can truly say I spend more time walking in His joy, peace and righteousness then I did before and I spend far less time worrying about the things that used to consume my thoughts.

God continues to prune me His SLA to me, so that I can bear more fruit and I continue to press in, keep the God Port open and seek first His kingdom, my SLA to Him!

Action Items

Reflect: What outcomes are you looking for right now in your life?

Why are you considering spending more time with God?

What are you hoping to gain?

Don't just list the spiritual list the tangible impact you are looking for (strategies to pay off debt, wisdom to go into business for your self, security and stability, improved health, a renewed hope, a better world, finances to build the kingdom, etc…).

Your time with God should not be focused on these outcomes but rather just spending time getting to know him however the results of that time will be very tangible and over the next few years you will see as you spend time with God the above items will get addressed.

Remember seek ye first …. and all other things….

We need to know what the other things are we want added so we know when they come!

This is our return on investment, our benchmark our measuring stick and our reward as we stay pressed into God.

Pray: *Lord I lift this reader up to you and ask that you bless them with your presence, that you encourage them with your voice and that you enlighten them through your word.*

Lord let them hear your voice even at this moment and know that you are with them and that you are calling them unto you, wooing them into the depths of who you are and who they are in you.

Lord bring them revelation even now into the things of you so that they will find joy in their time with you and be encouraged to persevere each day with you.

Continue this prayer with your own words to God, *Lord guide and direct me in this next season of spending more time with you.*

Lord direct me ...

Do: Write your commitment out to God right here as to the time you will meet with Him, the location you will meet Him at and the amount of time you will commit to Him starting today!

If your appointed time has already passed for the day then put this book down and take that time right now so you have your first day "under your belt" and you have victory!

If the time has not passed then set your alarm on your phone and make that first appointment!

_____
_____
_____

Write: Write out your thoughts below. How was this first appointment with God?

What was God showing you and speaking to you?

Just start writing and allow the Holy Spirit to flow through you. One word, one sentence, one paragraph whatever comes to mind.

Chapter Twelve

Real-time Streaming – What is God downloading?

Real-time streaming means you are listening or viewing the information at the same time as it is downloading from the server you are accessing it from.

In the early days of the internet when we were on dial up streaming was not even possible because the bandwidth wasn't sufficient.

You had to download the information first then play it from your local computer. This created a significant wait time between when you initially found the information you wanted and when you could actually begin viewing or listening to it.

Frustration often set in and many downloads were abandoned leaving the requested information behind.

Now with high-speed internet access people are streaming files all day long – watching television shows online, listening to radio stations, viewing video and audio files. Websites have video embedded on their home pages and people are spending hours watching You Tube!

The God Port is all about real-time streaming.

As you worship and praise God you receive His love and peace and joy real-time. As you read His word your eyes of your heart are enlightened at that moment.

As you connect to the God port and learn to stay connected you enjoy the high-speed real-time streaming from God, hearing His voice, His revelation, seeing visions and receiving understanding.

As I learned how to stay connected longer and was able to really begin experiencing this streaming, I began hearing the deeper truths of God from God. I am not talking about facts but truths, deep, revelatory truths about me, about God and about who I am in Him and Him in me.

Let's consider the difference between facts and truth.

A fact is defined as a piece of information about circumstances that exist or events that have occurred.

If you think about it facts can change over time. The fact is I lived in Cottage Grove, Oregon. The fact is I lived in Eugene Oregon. The fact was a circumstance that existed at a point in time but at a different point in time the fact was different, it had changed.

Now let's consider truth and what the bible says about truth.

> *"Jesus answered, I am the way and the truth and the life. No one comes to the Father except through me."* John 14:6
>
> *"You are a king, then!" said Pilate. Jesus answered, "You are right in saying I am a king. In fact, for this reason I was born, and for this I came into the world, to testify to the truth. Everyone on the side of truth listens to me."* John 18:37
>
> *"Jesus Christ is the same yesterday, today and forever."* Hebrews 13:8
>
> *"Every good and perfect gift is from above, coming down from the Father of the heavenly lights, who does not change like shifting shadows."* James 1:17

God never changes and Jesus is the same yesterday, today and forever. Jesus is truth and came to testify and bear witness to the truth.

We aren't talking facts here we are talking truth. We have the fullness of Christ in us through the Holy Spirit which means we have truth in us. Truth listens to His voice.

That is what we are hearing in the God port, that is the 24/7 streaming we are receiving…truth.

Truth that is unchanging, truth to understand God's word, truth to understand Kingdom principles, truth about our calling and election, truth about who we are, truth about the power that is within us from God, truth about heaven and hell, truth about truth.

It's a depth of understanding that is hard to describe, but those of you who spend time with God already know what I am referring to. Those of you that haven't pressed in to this degree may not understand it but you will as you begin opening your God port and letting truth begin to stream.

It's life-giving, and it removes doubt, unbelief, worry and stress and replaces it with peace, long suffering, kindness and all of the characteristics of Christ.

What is it like to walk in truth, to operate in truth, to make decisions in truth, to love your family in truth and to point others to truth?

How does this feel and how does this change your life?

When you begin walking in the truths of God, He shows you the lies of man, of this world, of the evil one. You are not viewing the world with your God port open and your truth lens on. When you begin to really believe, what you really believe is really real, you can walk in it and bring heaven to earth.

> *"My prayer is not that you take them out of the world but that you protect them from the evil one."* John 17:15

Here is a deeper truth; God wants to establish His Kingdom here on earth, He wants to establish the truths of Heaven here on earth through His children, His sheep, those who hear His voice.

We have been so busy believing that God is going to save us from this world by taking us to heaven but that's not what this verse says. He doesn't want to take us from this world; He wants to protect us from the evil one so we can establish His government here.

> *"For unto us a child is born, unto us a son is given; and the government is upon His shoulder; and His name shall be called Wonderful, Counselor, Mighty God, Everlasting Father, Prince of Peace."* Isaiah 9:6

What is the government of God, it is the Kingdom! A kingdom is a government; God's Kingdom is His government, perfect and without blemish and He wants to establish it here on earth!

> *From that time Jesus began to preach and say "Repent, for the Kingdom of Heaven is at hand."* Matthew 4:17

This was Jesus message to us, His first sermon, and the kingdom of Heaven is at hand. Remember Jesus is truth, he came to testify to it and these are His first words as He launched His ministry.

I realize these are not new verses, we have all read them and considered them and been taught about them. But have we really understood the depth of the truths in them?

And more have we modeled our lives around them?

As we begin to walk in the deeper truths of God we begin to see our calling and election, we begin to see our role in establishing heaven on earth, we begin to understand the part we play in the body of Christ to bring His government to fruition.

Jesus brought His government on His shoulders when He came, its here and real and waiting for God's people to establish it.

> *For through him we both have access to the Father by one Spirit.* Ephesians 2:18

We are all one in the Spirit and as we open our God port and stay connected we are all connected by that Spirit and can move mightily on this earth to bring His kingdom to reign.

Are you looking for your purpose in life, are you without hope, do you ever wonder what this is all for and why we are here? These are the questions that need God's truth to be answered, not the world's facts or the lies of the enemy.

Our purpose, our hope, our joy, peace and righteousness is found in our relationship with and truths from our Savior and Lord.

As we open the God port and begin to really believe what God says about who we are then we are transformed and we can begin transforming our family, our workplace, our community, our earthly governments and our world with these same truths.

We are called to establish God's kingdom here on earth and to be a part of His kingdom!

Instead of talking about the poor and the homeless we will be meeting their needs and feeding the widows and orphans at the city gates as we are called to.

We will be healing the sick and calling the lame to walk.

We will be walking in and acting according to the power that raised Christ from the dead that is in us!

Now that's something worth sacrificing time for don't you think. We are the answer to the world's problems, let's get started solving them according to what God has predestined us for!

Walking it Out

As I consider this last chapter and my final words to you in this book, I am prayerful that the words you have read have come from God and not me.

That through these words you have heard God speak to you and you have been refreshed as well as challenged to go further into the things of God, to press in and seek Him first and get two way communication going through the God Port.

I pray that somehow the technology analogies have helped you gain vision for what your walk with God looks like and what lies ahead for you as you learn to open your God Port.

I pray that you have received wisdom and revelation in what God is calling you to and that you will continue to pursue these glimpses that have come from God through the God Port.

I pray that God has used me in some small way to plant a seed or water one that had already been planted that you would want to grow in Him and begin to understand His truths and the depths of His love for you.

I pray God has been honored and glorified through the writing and publish and reading of this book and you would begin, resume or start anew your journey with Him and seeking your wide open connection with God.

Lastly I encourage you to start small, set a simple goal to spend consistent time with God every day.

If you aren't consistent with anytime with God like me then start very small, set aside 15 minutes the same time every day in a quiet place and begin seeking Him.

That's the same time every day, make an appointment with God and be faithful to it.

Go for consistency first then duration!

If you try to do too much too soon you will fail at both! Pray about it and commit to God your time together and He will be there every day, waiting for you to join Him, waiting for you to share your heart with Him and waiting to share His heart with you.

He's there waiting, wooing you, calling your name and wanting to give you the desires of your heart!

Action Items

Reflect: Has God ever shown you something about what you would do, who you would be, how the world would receive you?

Have you seen visions of your purpose and what God is calling you to?

Have you seen things and sensed your calling to achieve something but it hasn't happened yet?

Does your vision seem a long way off, unachievable, impossible? What are you passionate about?

What are the desires of your heart?

Pray: *Lord these are huge questions this reader is pondering and asking themselves. Lord show them how heaven sees them, show them those visions that they have seen before but given up on.*

Bring to mind the things that they were once passionate about but have not come to pass. Lord, ignite your purposes in their heart and allow their heart to leap with joy and excitement again as they ponder their calling and election, their passions and the desires of their heart.

Lord stir this reader for the things of you, for the assignment you have for them and deepen their understanding of their calling and election.

Continue this prayer with your own words to God, *Lord give me visions and dreams for the now and for that which is to come.*

Lord increase my capacity to believe and pursue the things you have shown me, the ...

Do: Write down one thing you feel the Lord is putting on your heart now, or has in the past, about something you are to accomplish or do.

My Vision:

_____
_____
_____
_____
_____
_____
_____
_____
_____
_____
_____
_____
_____
_____
_____
_____
_____
_____
_____
_____
_____
_____
_____
_____
_____

Write: Write out your thoughts below. What was God showing you and speaking to you?

Just start writing and allow the Holy Spirit to flow through you. One word, one sentence, one paragraph whatever comes to mind.

Afterword

As I read through The God Port once again I am truly amazed at the insights God has given me and the extent of my growth in Him over these last few years. The truths He has revealed to me have been simple yet profound.

I want to summarize a few of those simple truths here to make sure you are ready to embark on your journey of discovering God, opening The God Port and stepping into your calling and election.

First of all I embarked on my journey to hear God's voice and open The God Port because I wanted to know my calling and election. I knew God had a plan for me as His word says and I didn't feel I was moving forward in that plan.

I felt if I could hear His voice and understand Him, I would begin to understand what He has called me to here on earth.

Secondly, I knew I needed to spend more time, real time with God. He called me to a season of preparedness and spending time with Him was how I was to prepare for that which He was bringing me into (my calling and election).

Lastly, I just wanted more of God and the things of God. I was tired of the merry-go-round of life of working long hours, struggling financially and spiritually and the continual frustration of feeling I wasn't getting anywhere.

I wanted more of God, I wanted answers and I wanted to be the answer God had called me to be here on earth.

Quick Overview of opening your God Port:

1. Receive Christ as your savior. If you have not yet done this or are not sure you can pray this simple prayer:

    a. Lord I need you in my life, I believe that you raised Christ from the dead that I might be saved. I believe that Christ is your son and He was sent to die on the cross to save me from my sin.

    Lord forgive me of my sins and wrong doings and walk with me all the days of my life. I commit my life to you now and ask You to come into my heart and make me a new person in You. Amen.

    There it is finished, it is done. You are saved and a child of the King, the God most high!

    b. You may also read the bible verses on the second page of Chapter 11 again as a statement of your faith and say your own prayer as God leads you.

2. Spend time with God pressing in to who He is and who you are in Him

    a. Set aside a specific appointment time and place to meet with God daily

    b. Worshipping, praising, praying and giving thanks

    c. Reading the bible (His word) and letting it marinate in your spirit and believing what it says

    d. Being still before God

I would love to hear about your journey in opening the God Port. I have much more to learn and sharing our stories together will help each of us attain the things of God He has promised us.

You can go to my website, http://www.wendejones.com and sign up for my blog, provide comments and share your journey with other readers. There will also be a place for you to list your appointment time with God on the sign up so I can be praying for you and encouraging you on your journey as well.

As we get more appointment times I think it would be fun to display all the times people are spending with God and their locations to encourage each other and measure our accomplishments together, as well as encourage others to set their time with God.

I am specifically called to business and expanding the kingdom of God in the business arena and to establish His government here on earth. Whether you are called to this assignment as well or just figuring out how you can walk out your faith in your daily work place I will continue to develop resources to help with this journey.

I also have a list of other resources on my website that have helped me press into God and I think you will find these helpful as well. If you are a fellow business owner and want to learn more about running your business for Christ and what that means feel free to contact me for more information. It is time for the kings to unite together in Christ and transform the marketplace for His glory.

God called me to write this book as the beginning to set the stage for growing in Him, I sense there are many more to come and would love your thoughts and feedback on how I can continue to serve you in your calling to advance His kingdom here on earth.

Blessings,

Wende

About the Author

Wende Jones is a native Oregonian and has spent most of her life in the Pacific Northwest. She resides in the Beaverton area with her husband and her two daughters when they are not away at college, with her third daughter and grandchildren close by.

Wende is founder and CEO of Agile Northwest a software development company that focuses on building applications for the web and mobile devices for her clients that are spread out from Oregon to Washington DC. She has her credentials as a certified management consultant (CMC) and is a founding member of the Northwest Christian Chamber and serves on the Board.

Wende also serves on the board of directors for Nehemiah Project International Ministries because of her desire to see other Christian business owners excel and build sustainable and profitable kingdom businesses. Wende is an accomplished speaker and business consultant and enjoys educating CEO's and other top executives on technology and innovation. She speaks in Christian marketplace groups, conferences and venues to encourage, edify and train employees, leaders and business owners for their marketplace mission field. Whether CEO of a business or pastor of a church we are all called to minister to those God puts before us.

Wende truly believes that if we are all moving in our calling and election we are in full-time ministry in the sphere of influence we have been called to! She also enjoys ATV riding with her family and snowboarding in the winter when she has time.

Scripture Listing

All scripture is quoted from either the King James Bible or the New International Version (NIV)

Philippians 4:13
"I can do all things through Christ which strentheneth me."

Jeremiah 33:3
"Call to me and I will answer you and tell you great and unsearchable things you do not know."

Matthew 6:26
"Look at the birds of the air; they do not sow or reap or store away in barns, and yet your heavenly Father feeds them. Are you not much more valuable than they?"

I John 3:1
"How great is the love the Father has lavished on us, that we should be called children of God! And that is what we are! The reason the world does not know us is that it did not know him."

John 14:6-7
"I am the way and the truth and the life. No one comes to the Father except through me. If you really knew me, you would know my Father as well. From now on, you do know him and have seen him."

John 5:19
"I tell you the truth, the Son can do nothing by himself; he can do only what he sees his Father doing, because whatever the Father does the Son also does."

John 7:37-38
"If anyone is thirsty, let him come to me and drink. Whoever believes in me, as the Scripture has said, streams of living water will flow from within him."

John 7:37-38
"By this he meant the Spirit, whom those who believed in him were later to receive. p to that time the Spirit had not been given, since Jesus had not yet been glorified."

John 14:12
"I tell you the truth, anyone who has faith in me will do what I have been doing. He will do even greater things than these, because I am going to the Father."

John 16:7
"But I tell you the truth: It is for your good that I am going away. Unless I go away, the Counselor will not come to you; but if I go, I will send him to you."

John 14:26
"But the Counselor, the Holy Spirit, whom the Father will send in my name, will teach you all things and will remind you of everything I have said to you."

Psalm 139:17-18
"How precious to me are your thoughts, O God! How vast is the sum of them! Were I to count them, they would outnumber the grains of sand. When I awake, I am still with you."

Ephesians 1:18 - 19
"I pray also that the eyes of your heart maybe enlightened in order that you may know the hope to which he has called you, the riches of his glorious inheritance in the saints, and his incomparably great power for us who believe."

Matthew 13:10-11
"Why do you speak to the people in parables?" He replied, "The knowledge of the secrets of the kingdom of heaven has been given to you, but not to them.

Matthew 13:16-17
"But blessed are your eyes because they see, and your ears because they hear. For I tell you the truth, many prophets and righteous men longed to see what you see but did not see it, and to hear what you hear but did not hear it."

Romans 8:34
"…Christ Jesus, who died…more than that, who was raised to life…is at the right hand of God and is also interceding for us."

1 John 2:1
"My little children, these things write I unto you, that ye sin not. And if any man sin, we have an advocate with the Father, Jesus Christ the righteous."

John 14:15-17
"If you love me, you will obey what I command. And I will ask the Father, and he will give you another Counselor to be with you forever…the Spirit of truth. The world cannot accept him, because it neither sees him nor knows him. But you know him, for he lives with you and will be in you."

Romans 8:26
"In the same way, the Spirit helps us in our weakness. We do not know what we ought to pray for, but the Spirit himself intercedes for us with groans that words cannot express."

Matthew 16:19
""I will give you the keys of the kingdom of heaven; whatever you bind on earth will be bound in heaven, and whatever you loose on earth will be loosed in heaven."

Jeremiah 29:13
"You will seek me and find me when you seek me with all your heart."

Matthew 6:33
"But seek ye first the kingdom of God, and His righteousness; and all these things shall be added unto you."

Matthew 6:28-32
"And why do you worry about clothes? See how the lilies of the field grow. They do not labor or spin. Yet I tell you that not even Solomon in all his splendor was dressed like one of these. If that is how God clothes the grass of the field, which is here today and tomorrow is thrown into the fire, will he not much more clothe you. O you of little faith? So do not worry, saying 'What shall we eat? or 'What shall we drink?' or ' What shall we wear?' For the pagans run after all these things, and your heavenly Father knows that you need them."

Ephesians 1:19-21
"That power is like the working of his mighty strength, which he exerted in Christ when he raised him from the dead and seated him at his right hand in the heavenly realms, far above all rule and authority, power and dominion, and every title that can be given, not only in the present age but also in the one to come."

Psalm 22:3
"But thou art holy O thou that inhabitest the praises of Israel."

Psalm 139:14
"I praise you because I am fearfully and wonderfully made; your works are wonderful, I know that full well."

Luke 12:7
"Indeed, the very hairs of your head are all numbered. Don't be afraid; you are worth more than many sparrows."

2 Samuel 22:50
"Therefore I will praise you, O Lord, among the nations; I will sing praises to your name."

I Chronicles 23:5
"Four thousand are to be gatekeepers and four thousand are to praise the LORD with the musical instruments I have provided for that purpose."

Psalm 119:105
"Thy Word is a lamp unto my feet, and a light unto my path."

Romans 8:28-39
"And we know that in all things God works for the good of those who love him, who have been called according to his purpose. For those God foreknew he also predestined to be conformed to the likeness of his Son, that he might be the firstborn among many brothers. And those he predestined, he also called; those he called he also justified; those he justified, he also glorified. What, then, shall we say in response to this? If God is for us, who can be against us? He who did not spare his own Son, but gave him up for us all...how will he not also, along with him, graciously give us all things? Who will bring any charge against those whom God has chosen? It is God who justifies. Who is he that condemns? Christ Jesus, who died...more than that, who was raised to life...is at the right hand of God and is also interceding for us. Who shall separate us from the love of Christ? Shall trouble or hardship or persecution or famine or nakedness or danger or sword? As it is written:
For your sake we face death all day long; we are considered as sheep to be slaughtered.
No, in all these things we are more than conquerors through him who loves us. For I am convinced that neither death nor life, neither angels nor demons, neither the present nor the future, nor any powers, neither height nor depth nor anything else in all creation, will be able to separate us from the love of God that is in Christ Jesus our Lord."

Ephesians 1:18-21
"I pray also that the eyes of your heart may be enlightened in order that you may know the hope to which he has called you, the riches of his glorious inheritance in the saints, and his incomparably great power for us who believe.

That power is like the working of his mighty strength, which he exerted in Christ when he raised him from the dead and seated him at his right hand in the heavenly realms, far above all rule and authority, power and dominion, and every title that can be given, not only in the present age but also in the one to come."

Matthew 4:4
"Jesus answered, "It is written: 'Man does not live on bread alone, but on every word that comes from the mouth of God.'"

2 Peter 1:5-9
"For this very reason, make every effort to add to your faith goodness; and to goodness, knowledge; and to knowledge, self—control; and to self-control, perseverance; and to perseverance, godliness; and to godliness, brotherly kindness; and to brotherly kindness, love.
For if you posses these qualities in increasing measure, they will keep you from being ineffective and unproductive in your knowledge of our Lord Jesus Christ.
But if anyone does not have them, he is nearsighted and blind, and has forgotten that he has been cleansed from his past sins."

2 Corinthians 10:5
"We are destroying speculations and every lofty thing raised up against the knowledge of God and we are taking every thought captive to the obedience of Christ."

Ephesians 2:8-9
"For it is by grace you have been saved, through faith…and this not from yourselves, it is the gift of God…not by works, so that no one can boast."

Psalm 46:10
"Be still, and know that I am God."

Jeremiah 29:11-13
"For I know the plans I have for you," declares the Lord, "plans to prosper you and not to harm you, plans to give you hope and a future. Then you will call upon me and come and pray to me, and I will listen to you. You will seek me and find me when you seek me with all your heart."

I Corinthians 2:6-7
"We, do, however, speak a message of wisdom among the mature, but not the wisdom of this age or of the rulers of this age; who are coming to nothing. No, we speak of God's secret wisdom, a wisdom that has been hidden and that God destined for our glory before time began."

Ephesians 6:13
"Therefore put on the full armor of God, so that when the day of evil comes, you may be able to stand your ground, and after you have done everything, to stand."

Romans 12:2
"And be not conformed to this world: but be ye transformed by the renewing of your mind, that ye may prove what is that good, and acceptable, and perfect, will of God."

Romans 12:2
"Don't copy the behavior and customs of this world, but let God transform you into a new person by changing the way you think. Then you will learn to know God's will for you, which is good and pleasing and perfect."

Romans 14:17
"For the Kingdom of God is not a matter of eating and drinking, but of righteousness, peace and joy in the Holy Spirit."

Mark 16:15
"He sad to them, go into all the world and preach the good news to all creation."

II Peter 1:10-11
"Therefore, my brothers, be all the more eager to make your calling and election sure. For if you do these things, you will never fall and you will receive a rich welcome into the eternal kingdom of our Lord and Savior Jesus Christ."

Matthew 6:33
"But seek ye first the kingdom of God, and his righteousness; and all these things shall be added unto you."

Romans 10:9
"That if you confess with your mouth, "Jesus is Lord," and believe in your heart that God raised him from the dead, you will be saved."

1 John 1:9
"If we confess our sins He (Jesus Christ) is faithful and just to forgive us our sins and to cleanse us fro all unrighteousness."

John 1:12
"But as many as received him, to them gave he power to become the sons of God, even to them that believe on his name."

Revelation 3:20
"Behold I stand at your door and knock if any man hear my voice and open the door, I will come in to him and will sup with him and he with me."

Galatians 2:20
"I have been crucified with Christ and I no longer live, but Christ lives in me. The life I live in the body, I live by faith in the Son of God, who loved me and gave himself for me."

Romans 8:18
"I consider that our present sufferings are not worth comparing with the glory that will be revealed in us."

Ephesians 1:7-8
"In him we have redemption through his blood, the forgiveness of sins, in accordance with the riches of God's grace that he lavished on us with all wisdom and understanding."

1 John 3:1
"How great is the love the Father has lavished on us, that we should be called children of God! And that is what we are!"

John 14:6
"Jesus answered, I am the way and the truth and the life. No one comes to the Father except through me."

John 18:37
"You are a king, then!" said Pilate. Jesus answered, "You are right in saying I am a king. In fact, for this reason I was born, and for this I came into the world, to testify to the truth. Everyone on the side of truth listens to me."

Hebrews 13:8
"Jesus Christ is the same yesterday, today and forever."

James 1:17
"Every good and perfect gift is from above, coming down from the Father of the heavenly lights, who does not change like shifting shadows."

John 17:15
"My prayer is not that you take them out of the world but that you protect them from the evil one."

Isaiah 9:6
"For unto us a child is born, unto us a son is given; and the government is upon His shoulder; and His name shall be called Wonderful, Counselor, Mighty God, Everlasting Father, Prince of Peace."

Matthew 4:17
"From that time Jesus began to preach and say "Repent, for the Kingdom of Heaven is at hand."

Ephesians 2:18
"For through him we both have access to the Father by one Spirit."

Additional copies of this book may be purchased from www.WendeJones.com, and are available from your favorite online booksellers, as well.

Wende also conducts seminars and workshops for marketplace groups and churches, to inspire, encourage, and educate the body of Christ.

If you're interested in having Wende speak at your upcoming event please call (toll free) 1-866-739-6129 for availability and fees. You may email us regarding speaking and seminars at info@wendejones.com.

If you do not receive a response within 72 hours please call us, your email may have gotten held up in spam filters.

Made in the USA
Charleston, SC
21 January 2011